THE CASE FOR SOCIALISM

Socialist Workers Party

WHAT THE
SOCIALIST WORKERS PARTY
STANDS FOR

THE CASE FOR SOCIALISM

PAUL FOOT

Socialist Workers Party

The Case for Socialism / *Paul Foot*
First published July 1990. Second Printing August 1990.
Socialist Workers Party, PO Box 82, London E3.

ISBN 0 905998 74 X

Printed by Cox and Wyman Limited, Reading, England
Cover design by Roger Huddle

The *Socialist Workers Party* is part of an international grouping of socialist organisations:

Australia: *International Socialists*, GPO Box 1473N, Melbourne 3001
Belgium: *Socialisme International,* rue Lovinfosse 60, 4030 Grivegnée
Britain: *Socialist Workers Party,* PO Box 82, London E3
Canada: *International Socialists,* PO Box 339, Station E, Toronto, Ontario M6H 4E3
Denmark: *Internationale Socialister,* Ryesgade 8, 3, 8000 Århus C
France: *Socialisme International*, BP 189, 75926 Paris Cedex 19
Greece: *Organosi Sosialistiki Epanastasi*, PO Box 8161, 10010 Omonia, Athens.
Holland: *Groep Internationale Socialisten*, PO Box 9720, 3506 GR Utrecht.
Ireland: *Socialist Workers Movement,* PO Box 1648, Dublin 8
Norway: *Internasjonale Sosialister,* Postboks 5370, Majorstua, 0304 Oslo 3
United States: *International Socialist Organization,* PO Box 16085, Chicago, IL 60616
West Germany: *Sozialistische Arbeiter Gruppe,* Wolfgangstrasse 81, 6000 Frankfurt 1

Contents

Preface / 7

1: **The Foaming Wave** / 11

2: **The Full Tide** / 23

3 **The Tottering Thrones** / 43

4: **The Growing Wrath** / 55

5: **The New Eminence** / 69

6: **A World to win** / 75

Paul Foot is a long-standing member of the Socialist Workers Party. His previous books include **Why you should be a socialist** (1977) and **Red Shelley** (1980), among many others. He is a journalist and writes weekly columns for both the **Daily Mirror** and **Socialist Worker**.

PREFACE

THE THATCHER BUBBLE has burst. The long pretence that Margaret Thatcher and her ministers would bring new hope to the British people is at last exposed. The opinion polls show an astonishing swing to the Labour Party. A Labour government, which so recently seemed impossible, is now a real prospect.

The polls reflect a deep and angry shift of mood. The anger has flared up over the hated poll tax, which attacks everyone except the rich and has succeeded in uniting opposition to the Thatcher government for the first time. From the north of Scotland to the Isle of Wight, the biggest movement of civil disobedience in Britain this century has persuaded hundreds of thousands of people to resist the tax by not paying it. Their mood was summed up by a woman who defied a court summons for not paying her tax in terms which echoed the great protests of the poor, homeless and unemployed a hundred years ago:

> You're asking us for more money—us, the scum or rebels as you call us, who work hard for every penny. I want food in my stomach and clothes on my child's back.

In sudden disarray, the government tries to back off the poll tax. Huge sums of public money are sought as 'sweeteners' to bring the level of the tax down. But the new anger does not stop at the poll tax. It has become the symbol of all the other Tory plans and policies.

The huge privatisations which were meant to sweep away bureaucracy and bring down prices have set up new bureaucracies even more offensive and remote than their predecessors. Basic utilities such as water, electricity and gas have been delivered into the hands of greedy businesses which go about their profit-making without even a glance in the direction of parliament. The obsession with home ownership has resulted in a catastrophic fall in house-building and the steepest rise in homelessness in any decade for the past 60 years. The 'virtuous cycle' which Thatcher's chancellors have trumpeted ever since 1981—the idea that under new Tory guidance the economy would settle down to permanent and 'virtuous' growth—has been exposed as the same old stop-go, inspired by the same old virtues of squeeze and cut and grab. If workers in the early and mid-1980s were afraid to go on strike because of their mortgages, they are now afraid *not* to go on strike because of their mortgages. The great new property-owning democracy is revealed as a hoax: a transfer of ownership and power from landlords to moneylenders.

The poll tax completes the picture of a government hell-bent on further enriching the class which it represents at the expense of the people who create the wealth.

Margaret Thatcher herself has not been ashamed to describe her economic system as capitalism. Capitalism was a dirty word in the heydays of the 'fair-minded' Tories like Harold Macmillan and even Edward Heath. Thatcher, Ridley, Major and the others have dusted it down and pushed it out again. So the new fury against the Tory government is also a fury against capitalism. People do not want any more privatisation, any more high interest rates, any more homelessness, any more unemployment, any more ruthlessness and greed in high places. They don't want any more capitalism.

But what do they want? The traditional alternative to capitalism is socialism. Here people draw back, bemused. Capitalism is obviously detestable—but is not socialism detestable too? Is it not socialism that the people of Eastern Europe have just rejected in a series of political convulsions the like of which has not been seen in Europe since the kings departed after the First World War? Was it not socialism in the Union of Soviet Socialist Republics that plunged the common people of Russia into the most unspeakable poverty and deprivation? Is not socialism, on this evidence, a system of society which is even more bureaucratic, unfair and irresponsible than capitalism?

If so, is the best we can hope for just a muddled re-hash of what we have already? If socialism is what the people of Eastern Europe have overthrown in favour of capitalism, should we not accept that capitalism is here to stay, and try to reform it a little?

The point of this book is to rescue socialism from the awful caricature which has been made of it in Russia and Eastern Europe; to remember what the point of socialism was when it was first put forward; to restore to it its democratic essence; and to hold out a real socialist alternative to the defeatist apathy that now paralyses the left.

Forty years ago, George Orwell wrote a book about the future. It was titled **1984**. One feature of the terrifying society he imagined was that words were used by governments to mean their opposites. The chief purpose of the Ministry of Truth was to tell lies; of the Ministry of Love to erase even the slightest affection between human beings. Orwell's **1984** was and is a magnificent denunciation of a government which calls itself socialist while pursuing the most relentless campaign against socialism. But there is in the book no hope of change. Orwell's nightmare apparently goes on forever. There seems no possibility of resistance to the awful dictatorship he outlines.

The real 1984 has come and gone, and although things are bad they are nothing like as bad as Orwell suggested they might be. The regimes in Russia and Eastern Europe, which as a socialist he detested, have been overthrown by their own subjects. In the period immediately after the overthrow, of course, socialism is a hated word. It represents everything horrible about the old society. In the same way, if Orwell's **1984** society had been overthrown, words such as 'truth' and 'love' would have been hated words too. Gradually, however, words come back to their real meanings. Truth is the opposite of lies; love is the opposite of hate. And socialism is the opposite of capitalism and therefore entirely different from what it has been held up to be for 50 years and more.

The argument in this book is that socialism, real socialism, is the only alternative to capitalism; and it is still worth fighting for.

1: THE FOAMING WAVE

'All these conditions cannot be fulfilled by pamphlets and leaflets, but only by the living political school, by the fight and in the fight, in the continuous course of the revolution.'

—*Rosa Luxemburg.*

'EVER SINCE the beginning of time,' says a disembodied voice over a picture of a spinning globe at the start of Cecil B de Mille's film **Samson and Delilah**, 'man has striven to achieve a democratic state on earth.' That is probably putting it a little high (especially as the voice goes on to assert: 'such a man was Samson'), but there is some truth in it. For thousands of years there have been oppressors and oppressed; rich and poor; powerful and weak; and through all that time the first group have robbed the second. During all that time, too, people at the bottom have dreamt of a world where there would be no oppression but where people would live in peace without being robbed. Most of these utopias were in heaven. The few that ever existed on earth were always in isolation from the real world.

In feudal times, there was less than enough to go round: nothing like enough, for instance, to feed everyone. If anyone was to progress at all from the lowest form of human life, they had to turn themselves into rulers, seize the land and steal a surplus from the people who tilled it. Obviously they could not do this as individuals. They had to band together into classes, to pool their resources with others so that they could more effectively rob the majority, or go to war with other rulers in other parts of the world.

The word 'socialism' was first used in France after the Great Revolution which finally put paid to feudalism. Capitalism, the system which emerged, completely changed the economic and social environment. It brought men and women together, to co-operate with one another in production. Feudal backwardness and isolation were replaced by capitalist progress and growth.

The wealth which was produced under the new system was so enormous that there was, quite suddenly, enough to go round. For the first time it was possible for people to imagine a society where everyone could live in relative equality: where there was no need for exploiters and exploited, and where the means of production could be owned not by marauding individuals but by society. Workers were cooperating to produce; why then should they not extend that cooperation to deciding what they produced, and to whom and how it was distributed?

In such a cooperative society, production could be planned to fit everyone's needs. Distribution, exchange—everything else in society—could be organised socially. It followed that in socialist society, there would be no need for anyone to fight anyone else. There would be more than enough for everyone, and it would be distributed not on the basis of who had the strongest army or who could make the biggest gun, but on the basis of who needed most.

These simple socialist ideas were first put around by people later called 'utopians', who argued that such a society would emerge if people thought about it and understood it. The strength of the idea alone, they argued, would persuade the capitalists either to surrender their property or to organise it in the interests of everyone, including their own workers.

One of the earliest socialists in Britain was Robert Owen. He was a wealthy man who put his socialist ideas into practice by organising his mill in New Lanark, Scotland, so that workers worked decent hours for reasonable wages. Education and medical care were provided for them and their families.

New Lanark was not a bad place to work. But it was completely isolated. To Robert Owen's anguish, every other employer preferred old-fashioned Christian values of robbery and greed. New Lanark staggered on in isolation, until the iron grip of the employers in every other part of Scotland strangled it.

The utopian socialists were put to flight in the 1840s by a young German revolutionary called Karl Marx. Just as socialism is being 'written off' by all important people today, so in his lifetime

(1818 to 1883) and ever since, Karl Marx has been 'written off' by each successive generation of politicians and intellectuals. At his funeral in Highgate, North London, the graveside oration was made by his collaborator and friend, Frederick Engels. In a short, simple speech Engels summed up Marx's enormous contribution to civilisation. Just as Darwin discovered that mankind had developed from animals—the law of evolution—so Marx discovered

> the simple fact, hitherto concealed by an overgrowth of ideology, that mankind must first of all eat and drink, have shelter and clothing, before it can pursue politics, science, religion and art; and that therefore the production of the immediate material means of life and consequently the degree of economic development... form the foundation upon which the forms of government, the legal conceptions, the art and even the religious ideas of the people concerned have been evolved... instead of vice versa as had hitherto been the case.

Marx argued that all human history was dominated by a tussle for the wealth between classes, one of which took the wealth, and used it to exploit the others. As science and technology developed, so one exploiting class was replaced by another that used the resources of society more efficiently. The necessity for exploitation, he observed, had ended with capitalism. If the working class, the masses who cooperate to produce the wealth, could seize the means of production from the capitalist class, they could put an end to exploitation forever and run society on the lines of the famous slogan: 'From each according to his abilities, to each according to his needs.'

Famous people throughout history have scoffed at Marx as a remote academic, who wrote for intellectuals and not for the masses. This entirely misses the main inspiration of Marx's life. Here is Engels again, by the graveside:

> Marx was before all else a revolutionary. His real mission in life was to contribute in one way or another to the overthrow of capitalist society and of the forms of government which it had brought into being... Fighting was his element.

When Marx's daughter Eleanor asked him for his favourite character in history, Marx replied immediately: 'Spartacus'. The fighting spirit of the slave revolutionary against the Roman Empire inspired Marx's enthusiasm for the class struggle in his own time. It was, as he put it, all very well for people to understand the rotten world they lived in. The point, however, was to change it.

How could it be changed? It certainly was no good just thinking about a new society, or trying to attract others to it by example. Exploiters who amassed their power and wealth by robbing workers were not sentimental or namby-pamby about it. They would hold on to their wealth and power, if they had to, by force. They would never surrender that power and wealth, however intellectually or morally unjustifiable it was. It was up to the exploited class—the working class—to seize the means of production in a revolution. No one could do it for them. Socialism could not be introduced by utopians, dictators, benevolent or otherwise, or by reforming intellectuals and politicians. The first precondition for socialism was that the wealth of society had to be taken over by the workers.

Marx faced up squarely to an argument which is common enough a 150 years later. How, he was asked, can you expect the workers to change society? Are they not the most damaged victims of class rule? Are they not religious, racist, nationalist, dirty and violent?

Marx reacted angrily to this abuse. He had spent a lot of his time with the workers of Paris when he was exiled there in the late 1840s. He knew that there were among the workers people of outstanding courage and self-sacrifice, and that workers' attitudes could quickly change when they took part in collective struggle such as a strike.

But he was not, as so many middle-class socialists can be, a worker-worshipper. He realised that an exploiting society corrupts everyone in it: the exploited as well as the exploiters. Not to put too fine a point on it, capitalist society covered everything in shit. And that was the best argument of all for a workers' revolution; he wrote:

> This revolution is necessary not only because the ruling class cannot be overthrown in any other way, but also

because the class overturning it can only in a revolution succeed in ridding itself of all the muck of ages and become fitted to found society anew.

While reforms are carried out in the name of workers by someone from on high, the muck of ages sticks to them. The hierarchies created by exploitation encourage even the most degraded and exploited worker to seek someone else whom he can insult and bully as he himself is insulted and bullied. In such circumstances, workers will take pride in things of which there is nothing to be proud: the colour of their skin, their sex, nationality, birthplace or God. These are selected for them by custom, inheritance or superstition, and have nothing to do with their abilities or characters. They are the muck of ages. How are they to be shaken off? Is someone else to do it for the workers? Or should they do it themselves, by organising their producing power, their own strikes, demonstrations and protests?

When people asked Marx for blueprints of a socialist society, he steadfastly refused to supply them. He would not, he said, 'provide them with recipes for their cookbooks'. The question 'what is socialism?' is, he argued, inextricably entwined with another: how can socialism be achieved? No socialist utopia was worth the paper it was written on if its authors expected the workers to be passive while the utopia was achieved. The seed of the new society could only be sown in the struggle against the old one. The only way labour could be emancipated from capital was by the active struggle from below—and a struggle from below could not and would not be set in motion from above.

In 1864 Marx wrote the articles for the first International Working Men's Association. The first clause started: 'Considering that the emancipation of the working classes must be conquered by the working classes themselves...' That clause was written on the cards of every member of the International. It was the very lynchpin of Marx's socialism.

Seven years after the International was formed, the people of Paris, led by the working class in the city, rose, threw off the muck of ages, and set up their own administration: the Paris Commune. It only lasted a couple of months, when it was drowned in the most ferocious ruling-class slaughter. Marx responded at once with one of the most powerful political pamphlets in all history, which he read out loud to a meeting of the International's executive. The Commune's outstanding achievement, he said, was the self-emancipation of the working class:

> They have taken the actual management of the revolution into their own hands and found at the same time, in the case of success, the means to hold it in the hands of the people itself; displacing the state machinery of the ruling class by a governmental machinery of their own. This is their ineffable crime!

What kind of a society did they set up? 'The Commune,' Marx reported,

> was formed of the municipal councillors, chosen by universal suffrage in the various wards of the town, responsible and revocable at short terms. The Commune was to be a working, not a parliamentary body, executive and legislative at the same time. Instead of continuing to be the agent of the central government, the police was at once stripped of its political attributes and turned into the responsible and revocable agent of the Commune. So were the officials of all other branches of the administration. From the members of the Commune downwards, the public service had to be done at workmen's wages. The vested interests and the representation allowances of the high dignitaries of state disappeared along with the high dignitaries themselves...

The Commune worked. That was no surprise to Marx, for he saw in the Commune 'the produce of the struggle of the producing against the appropriating class'. It was the living expression of the self-emancipation of the working class.

The other aspect of the Commune which appealed to Marx was its democracy. He liked the fact that it was elected, and the way it was elected. The Commune was infinitely more democratic than any parliamentary democracy the world has known. The executive, as well as the political assembly, the judiciary, the police, education, science, industry and finance—all these became, in the two most consistent words in the pamphlet, 'responsible' and 'revocable'.

Marx had seen how workers chose their own representatives in their workplaces. They chose the people they most trusted for positions which held no privilege and no extra wages. Those elected were subject to constant questioning and, if they did not carry out their mandates, to recall. That was a natural way for people to choose their representatives. It brought the representatives close to their electors. It was a democracy which the common people could trust.

The caricature of Marx painted by his enemies over the past 130 years is that he was a tyrant with no interest in democracy. Edmund Wilson, in his famous introduction to his book **To the Finland Station**, which is about the growth of socialist ideas from the French to the Russian revolution, wrote that Marx 'was incapable of imagining democracy'. Well, Marx wasn't terribly interested in imagining anything. But what attracted him to politics in the first place was a loathing for tyranny and a yearning for democracy. In his youth he was known by everyone as 'an extreme democrat'.

Marx himself wrote how his passionate longing for democracy brought him to socialism. No democracy was worth its name if industry, finance, law and the armed services stayed in the hands of a completely unelected and irresponsible minority. The democratic element in such a democracy was certain to be corrupted and eventually squeezed out. For a democracy to deserve the name, labour had to emancipate itself and, as part of the process, democratise all the areas of society which were constipated by class rule. 'Democracy,' wrote Engels in 1845, 'nowadays is communism... democracy has become the principle of the masses... the proletarian parties are entirely right in inscribing the word "democracy" on their banners.'

The point about socialism is that it would replace a hierarchical, bureaucratic and undemocratic society—capitalism—with a genuine democracy in which the working people controlled their own representatives, and the representatives acted accordingly.

These elements—the self-emancipation of the working class through their own struggle and the democratic society which follows such emancipation—are the heart of socialism. Without them, socialism is dead. All the other features of a socialist society—the planned economy, for instance—depend on a self-emancipated working class and a real democracy. A socialist economy cannot be planned for workers unless the workers are involved in that plan. It took a plan to build the pyramids, but the slaves who built them are not reported to have rejoiced that this new planning brought anything but a life and death under the whip. Like everything else about socialism, the plan depends on who are the planners and how they got there. Socialism depends upon control from below, and control from below can never be brought about from above.

Marx died in 1883, when socialism was still a subject for minorities. He did not live to see the huge growth of the German Social Democratic Party, which claimed it was based on his principles.

As long as the ruling class in Germany withheld the vote and suppressed the growing labour movement, it seemed obvious to most people that socialism could come only through a revolution. But as more and more workers were given the right to vote, and as the trade unions grew into enormous and influential organisations, most socialists started to sing a different tune. In 1898, Eduard Bernstein wrote a pamphlet, which was instantly denounced by other Social Democratic leaders—though they secretly agreed with it. Bernstein argued that the vote and the unions changed the socialist perspective. With the vote and the unions, the working class could be emancipated without a revolution: by getting socialists elected to parliament and there passing laws to change the system. This could be done without antagonising the government or the state, and without calling on people to risk anything, or indeed to do anything or to think anything. All they would have to do was vote.

Bernstein's book provoked a furious response from another leading member of the German Social Democratic Party: Rosa Luxemburg. Her central point was that Bernstein's argument was not just an argument about means and ends—but about socialism itself:

> People who pronounce themselves in favour of the method of legislative reform in place of and in contradistinction to the conquest of political power and social revolution, do not really choose a more tranquil, calmer and slower road to the same goal, but a different goal. Instead of taking a stand for the establishment of a new society, they take a stand for the

> surface modification of the old society. Our programme becomes not the realisation of socialism, but the reform of capitalism.

Capitalism, she argued, was not made by laws, and would not be undone by laws. It was an economic system, which had to be replaced by another economic system.

The worst part of Bernstein's proposals was that they left the masses passive: unable to throw off the muck of ages, and so unable to change society. This passivity would, she predicted, make it difficult for the Bernstein reformers to carry out even their most marginal reforms. But the main point about them was that by changing the means of getting socialism, they changed the meaning of socialism itself.

Rosa Luxemburg's attack on Bernstein—it was titled **Social Reform or Revolution**—was published in 1900. She returned to the attack six years later in another even more remarkable pamphlet called **The Mass Strike**. Its inspiration was the Russian revolution of 1905. She watched with increasing excitement as hundreds of years of tyranny in Russia were brought to a halt, not by gradual reforms or by the resurfacing of the old society by wise men at the top, but by the most cataclysmic upheaval from below. She contrasted the slow, steady, ordered march of the German trade unions, through their conferences, sporting associations, libraries, offices and marble halls, with the uprising of Russian workers, many of whom were not even members of trade unions:

> While the guardians of the German trade unions for the most part fear that the organisations will fall in pieces in a revolutionary whirlwind like rare porcelain, the Russian revolution shows us the exactly opposite picture: from the whirlwind and the storm, out of the fire and glow of the mass strike and the street fighting, rise again, like Venus from the foam, fresh, young, powerful, buoyant trade unions.

Better by far a group of raw workers in struggle than a committee of long-organised trade unionists solemnly selecting candidates for a parliamentary party. The pamphlet throbs with the living spirit of the self-emancipation of workers in struggle: the same spirit which had excited Marx at the time of the Commune. Against the passive piecemeal progress of Bernstein she counterposed the 'living political school', the 'pulsating flesh and blood', the 'foaming wave' of the workers in struggle, breaking down the wall of capitalism and in the process purging themselves of the muck of ages.

This argument between Eduard Bernstein and Rosa Luxemburg has been going on in different tones all through this century. The enormous majority of socialists and even Marxists have taken Bernstein's side. The reformists offered real reforms, many of which affected the real lives of working people. They offered a clear instrument by which the reforms could be carried out: by electing Labour or social-democratic governments and passing new laws in parliaments; and they demanded from the masses very little —only the vote. How much more 'sensible' and 'practical' it seemed to get socialism through peaceful parliaments than by revolutions which were vague in theory and dangerous in practice!

A perfect example of the Bernstein method in action was a motion in the British House of Commons which was debated on 20 March and 16 July 1923:

> That, in view of the failure of the capitalist system to adequately utilise and organise natural resources and productive power, or to provide the necessary standard of life for vast numbers of the population, and believing that the cause of this failure lies in the private ownership and control of the means of production and distribution, this House declares that legislative effort should be directed to the gradual supersession of the capitalist system by an industrial and social order based on public ownership and democratic control of the instruments of production and distribution.

The debate was ended by the leader of the Labour Party, Ramsay Macdonald, with the words: 'I am in favour of socialism.' He lost the vote in the House of Commons that day: 121 MPs voted for socialism; 368 for capitalism.

But a few months later Ramsay Macdonald got his chance. He led the Labour Party to its first election victory, and became prime minister. His government lasted less than a year. It did nothing.

Macdonald's Labour Party was returned to office again in 1929, pledged to rid Britain forever of the 'scourge of unemployment'. A million people were out of work. Two years of Labour policies later, there were three million out of work, and Macdonald joined the Tories in a National Government.

Labour and social-democratic governments have been elected throughout Europe all this century. Their model has been Bernstein's—to enact socialist measures through parliament. When every one of these governments left office, capitalism was stronger and socialism weaker. As Rosa Luxemburg had predicted, the enthusiasm for gradual means has gradually erased the ends. No Labour or social-democratic party now puts forward motions in parliament to get socialism by 'gradual supersession', or by any other means for that matter. Instead, they have come to admit that they do not want socialism at all. They prefer, as Rosa Luxemburg predicted, a 'reformed capitalism'—a 'different goal'.

When socialism lost its soul—the self-emancipation of the working class, and a democratic society organised from below—it ceased to be socialism, and became something completely different.

With these dismal consequences, the Bernsteins won the argument for most of the 20th century. But they did not get it all their own way. In that debate in the House of Commons in 1923, the MP for Motherwell, John Newbold, embarrassed the Labour Party leaders with a remarkable forecast:

> Apparently, nothing is going to ensue, because we have been informed that the Labour Party is not in favour of the use of force. Consequently, they have told the governing class that they will not have their property taken away. Nothing further will happen except a series of resolutions, and the governing class will say: 'We will keep our capital in our pocket for nothing is going to occur.'

John Newbold, though in a minority of two in the whole House of Commons, was well equipped to speak up for the soul of socialism: for the tradition of Marx, Engels and Rosa Luxemburg. He was a member of the Communist Party and a supporter of the Russian Revolution.

2: THE FULL TIDE

'How far they had soared, these *Bolsheviki*, from a despised and hunted sect less than four months ago, to this supreme place, the helm of great Russia in the full tide of insurrection!'

—*John Reed,* **Ten days that shook the world.**

IN THE Russian revolution of 1905, which so inspired Rosa Luxemburg, the workers in the Russian cities created a new form of political power. Up to that time, the limit of democracy for most oppressed people of the world was a parliament, elected by universal suffrage. Under the tyranny of the Tsars, of course, no worker or peasant in Russia had the vote. Nevertheless, in the great upheaval of the 1905 revolution, the Russian working class reached out for something far more democratic than an elected parliament. On their own, without any 'blueprints', they formed *soviets*, or workers' councils, based on the democracy of the Paris Commune.

The leaders of the *soviets* were 'responsible and revocable' at all times. They earned exactly the same as the people they represented. And they found it easy and natural to combine with other *soviets* and so establish a network of democratic power the like of which had never been seen before, even during the Commune, and certainly has not been seen since.

The 1905 revolution was crushed by the Tsar and his army. In the twelve years which followed, he reluctantly made concessions on voting. For a few years both wings of the Russian Social Democratic Party—Bolsheviks (revolutionary) and Mensheviks (reformist)—had seats in the Russian parliament, the Duma. But *soviets* of all kinds were banned with the utmost severity. The short-lived *soviets* of 1905 had sown more terror in the hearts of propertied people than all the movements for parliamentary reform put together.

In February 1917, the Russian workers and peasants rose again in another, even more furious revolution. The First World War had inflicted on them greater suffering than anywhere else in Europe. There seemed no end to the war, nor to the ruthless class policies of the Tsar and his advisers. In a trice, the February revolution overthrew forever the Tsarist tyranny. It was replaced by a provisional government which promised a parliament and continued the war. At the same time, workers, soldiers and peasants set up *soviets* on a far greater scale than in 1905.

In the ensuing tumultuous nine months, the two forms of power—the old state and the new *soviets*—operated side by side.

The provisional government, under its prime minister, Kerensky, staggered aimlessly under the huge burden of the war, which it was determined to continue. Kerensky was forced again and again into the policies which had been carried out by the Tsar. Quickly, the popularity of the provisional government started to disappear. The people, both in the cities and in the countryside, clamoured for more. This clamour was not often heard by the government. The anger and aspirations of the people, and especially of the working class, expressed itself in the political organisations which more closely represented them: the *soviets*.

When the *soviets* were first elected in February, they were dominated by the Social Revolutionaries, whose strength was in the countryside among the peasants, and the Menshevik wing of the Social Democratic Party. The Mensheviks argued that the job of the *soviets* was to advise and pressurise the provisional government, not to replace it. They treated the *soviets* as sounding boards, glorified trade unions where people could express their opinions and pass them on to the real power: the provisional government.

The Bolsheviks, however, raised the slogan 'All power to the *soviets*!' For several months they remained in the minority. In June 1917, at the First All-Russian Congress of Soviets, the peasant-based Social Revolutionaries had 283 delegates; the Mensheviks 248 and the Bolsheviks 105.

The *soviets'* feeling that they were subordinate to the provisional government was reflected in the resolutions they passed. Even in the advanced areas of the two main cities, Moscow and Petrograd, these resolutions flattered, begged or scolded the provisional government.

The mood changed, however, and it changed swiftly. Rising inflation, the increased horror of the war and the hesitancy and impotence of the provisional government stung the workers into action. In the factories, they started to take control of production. Social problems to do with housing, sanitation, fuel and food were increasingly dealt with not at the town hall, or by the government or civil service, but by the local *soviet*. The pendulum of power, which had been heavily weighted towards Kerensky, swung instead to the *soviets*.

At first this was reflected simply in 'practical' decisions: a house repair here, a bonus claim settled there. But as even these came up against the real economic power of the employers and the landlords, the discussions and demands of the *soviets* became increasingly political. In August, the employers and landlords backed a military coup whose aim was to destroy the *soviets*. The workers were armed and the coup was defeated.

The result was a staggering increase in the influence of the *soviets* and of the Bolshevik wing inside them. First the *soviets* started passing Bolshevik resolutions. Then they went over to the Bolsheviks. On 31 August, the *soviet* in Petrograd, then Russia's biggest city, passed a Bolshevik resolution for the first time. It called for workers' control of industry, immediate negotiations to end the war, confiscation of the large estates and a government of the 'revolutionary proletariat and peasantry'.

These slogans were quickly whittled down to three words: Peace, Bread, Land. In another two weeks, the Bolsheviks won control of the *soviets* in Petrograd and Moscow. By the time the All-Russian Congress of Soviets met again (in October) the whole political situation in Russia had changed. This time the Bolsheviks had 390 delegates, the Social Revolutionaries 160, the Mensheviks only 72.

This change in the *soviets* was repeated in the even more remarkable figures for Bolshevik Party membership. What had been, in John Reed's words, a 'despised and hunted sect' became, almost overnight, a mass party. Between April and October Bolshevik Party membership in Petrograd rose from 16,000 to 43,000. In Moscow, membership in March was only 600; by August it was 15,000. In Kiev membership was up from 200 to 4000; in Ekaterinburg from 40 to 1700 and in the small industrial town of Ivanovo-Voznesensk, where there were ten Bolshevik members in March, in August there were 5440.

While the provisional government stayed the same, talked the same, behaved the same, the workers of Russia had entirely changed their tune. These changes took place in conditions of great social turmoil: constant strikes, demonstrations, street meetings and debates. What was happening (without Kerensky really noticing) was the self-emancipation of the working class.

In April 1917, Lenin, the leader of the Bolsheviks, came back to Russia from exile. He immediately embarked on a revolutionary strategy to replace the Kerensky government with a socialist one. He found that the paralysis of the provisional government had affected even the leaders of his own party. Many leading Bolsheviks saw the provisional government as the highest form of democracy for which anyone could hope; therefore they adapted their politics to supporting the government. Lenin replied at once—and he kept saying it all through the tempestuous months which followed—that it was possible to create a more advanced form of democracy than parliament:

> Bourgeois democracy, although a great historical advance in comparison to medievalism, always remains, and under capitalism is bound to remain, restricted, truncated, false and hypocritical, a paradise for the rich and a snare and deception for the exploited, for the poor... deceit, violence, corruption, mendacity, hypocrisy and oppression of the poor is hidden beneath the civilised, polished and perfumed exterior of modern bourgeois democracy.

Although Lenin was as vitriolic a polemicist as any writer in history, he did not rely on destructive abuse. Against the 'polished and perfumed' parliaments, he proposed real, live instruments of democratic political power. In the summer of 1917 he took time off from revolutionary activity to write a pamphlet, **The State and Revolution**, which again addressed the question: is there a way forward from this corrupt and paralytic provisional government? If we junk it, are we not junking any hope of what little democracy we have?

Lenin replied that the problem with parliaments was not that they were democratic, but that they were not democratic enough. He restated the socialism which had been emphasised by Marx, Engels and Rosa Luxemburg:

> The way out of parliamentarism is to be found, of course, not in the abolition of the representative institutions and the elective principle, but in the conversion of the representative institutions from mere 'talking shops' into working bodies.

The problem with parliaments was that they did the talking while someone else did the doing:

> The actual work of the state is done behind the scenes, and is carried out by the departments, the chancellories and their staffs.

These people who carried out 'the actual work of the state' were not elected, not responsible, not revocable. They directly represented the people with property, the capitalist class. Thus the elected representatives chattered in a language whose special purpose was 'the fooling of the common people' while the 'actual work of the state' went on robbing the common people.

The thousands of intellectuals then and since who abused Lenin as a 'tyrant' and a 'dictator' cannot have read **The State and Revolution**, which again and again repeats that socialism and democracy are indivisible.

'Without representative institutions we cannot imagine a democracy, even a proletarian democracy,' wrote Lenin. Representative institutions were the life blood of socialism, and socialists had to ensure that their institutions were truly representative, truly democratic, truly responsible and revocable, and above all secure from the corrupt and cloying attention of an exploiting class. That class managed to stay in control in spite of elected parliaments because it controlled the machinery of the state: the civil service, the army, the police, the media, the law. If any genuine democracy was to be set up, if society was to be governed by genuinely representative institutions, then that state had to be destroyed and a new one entirely rebuilt in the image of a democratic and egalitarian society:

> We must reduce the role of the state officials to that of simply carrying out our instructions; they must be responsible, revocable, moderately paid...

It followed that democracy and the representative institutions, which were the foundation of socialism, were not inscriptions on blackboards for the workers passively to read and understand. They had to be created in struggle. Lenin writes, as Marx did, of 'the birth of the new society from the old'.

The State and Revolution part one was published in August 1917. There was never a part two. In December 1917, Lenin added an 'afterword' to yet another edition, explaining that he was for the moment otherwise engaged. 'It is more pleasant and more useful to live through a revolution than to write about it,' he wrote.

Lenin's outline of the emancipation of the working class was and is ten times more powerful because it was written while the workers were emancipating themselves. Throughout the century, it has risen and fallen in popularity just as the masses have risen and fallen. During the Portuguese revolution of 1974, for instance, a Lisbon newspaper published a 'best-sellers' list. Harold Robbins' novel **The Carpet-Baggers** was eighth. First was Lenin's **The State and Revolution**.

The October revolution in Russia, in which the *soviets*, under the leadership of the Bolshevik Party, asserted their power over the parliament, sacked the government and established what Lenin called 'the socialist order', is the greatest event in all human history.

The world was turned upside down. Control and administration of society was no longer exclusive to a few. It was no longer necessary to be rich to be responsible. The wonder of the revolution was not so much in its festivities, in its cheering crowds and emotional renderings of the *Internationale*. It was in its democratic spirit. The talents, capacities, emotions and confidences of the common people, which are blunted and corrupted in an exploiting society, were unleashed. John Reed, an American journalist who had the luck to be in Russia during that October, wrote a book to celebrate the **Ten days that shook the world**:

> Then the Talk, beside which Carlyle's 'flood of French speech' was a mere trickle. Lectures, debates, speeches—in theatres, circuses, school-houses, clubs, *soviet* meeting

rooms, union headquarters, barracks... Meetings in the trenches at the Front, in village squares, factories... What a marvellous sight to see the Putilov factory pour out its forty thousand to listen to Social Democrats, Socialist Revolutionaries, Anarchists, anybody, whatever they had to say as long as they would talk! For months in Petrograd, and all over Russia, every street corner was a public tribune. In railway trains, street-cars, always the spurting up of impromptu debate, everywhere...

The 'socialist order' set up after October was not a democratic paradise—far from it. There was a constant jumble of mistakes and counter-mistakes, uneasy relationships between different power brokers, lapses into bureaucracy. The capitalist governments outside Russia did not want their world turned upside down, and they immediately set out to destroy the Russian revolution by force. They redoubled their military effort on the Russian front, and financed army after army of angry Russian émigrés outraged that 'their property', which they had amassed in centuries of plunder, had been confiscated by the Bolshevik upstarts. The very word 'Bolshie' was adopted in different languages to describe the uncooperative child who refuses to obey its parents.

The war and the economic blockade made it impossible for the new socialist republic to realise the main economic aim of socialism: plenty. For the first few years after the revolution, there was widespread starvation and privation. Production slumped to less than half what it had been before the war and before the revolution. The remarkable feature of those first few years, however, is how much the new society was able to survive, develop and emancipate itself. That it did so at all was entirely due to the workers who had created the revolution, and their determination not to let go of the democracy they had won. 'I calculated,' Lenin explained,

> solely and exclusively on the workers, soldiers and peasants being able to tackle better than the officials, better than the police, the practical and difficult problems of increasing the production of foodstuffs and their better provision, the better provision of soldiers etc.

In January 1918, he told the first post-revolutionary All-Russian Congress of Soviets:

> In introducing workers' control, we knew it would take some time before it spread to the whole of Russia, but we wanted to show that we recognised only one road—changes from below. We wanted the workers themselves to draw up, from below, the new principles of economic conditions.

The revolution was increasingly beleaguered by civil war, famine and a failure of production, but it was saved from instant defeat by this emphasis on control from below. When sacrifices had to be made, they were made even-handedly. The poor were treated as priorities, the privileged expropriated. Wonders were performed far more remarkable than in war or natural disaster. Because millions of newly emancipated people felt that this was their society which they had created, they stubbornly defended it literally to the last drops of sweat and blood. Victor Serge, a French socialist who joined in the Russian revolution with every fibre of his mind and body, wrote:

> In spite of this grotesque misery, a prodigious impulse was given to public education. Such a thirst for knowledge sprang up all over the country that new schools, adult courses, universities and Workers' Faculties were formed everywhere. Innumerable fresh initiatives laid open the teaching of unheard-of, totally unexplored domains of learning.

The education minister, Lunacharsky, lectured to thousands of starving, freezing workers—on Greek drama. Museums, enriched with works of art confiscated from great private estates, were somehow kept open and visited by hundreds of thousands of people who had never before heard of a museum. Theatres, libraries, ballet companies, scientific laboratories—all managed to defy the cold and dark and hunger.

At the new ministry of social welfare, under the first woman government minister in the whole history of the world—Alexandra Kollontai—they set up a new system of benefits which put the poorest first. Maternity benefit was introduced for the first time anywhere in the world. Old dark laws preventing abortion and divorce were swept aside in a series of revolutionary decrees. For the first time, abortion was free, safe and on demand.

Somehow, the new society clung to its democracy. Elections were still held to the *soviets*, whose members were indeed responsible and revocable. Victor Serge wrote:

> In the years of the greatest peril the *soviets* and the central executive committee of the *soviets* included left social revolutionaries (who were part of the government in the first nine months), Maximalists, anarchists, Menshevik social democrats, and even right social revolutionaries—the latter unalterable enemies of the new power. Far from fearing discussion, Lenin seeks after it, having Martov and Dan, who had been expelled from the All-Russian executive, invited to come to take the floor. He feels that he has something to learn from their merciless criticism.

In spite of cries from all sides to keep the Mensheviks out of political activity, to 'shut them up' until at least the civil war was won, the Mensheviks went on playing an active part in the political life of the new society. Throughout 1920 they had party offices and a club in Moscow. They even led a strike in Moscow in the summer of 1918. And they kept winning seats (though a minority of them) in the *soviets*: in 1920 they won 46 seats in the Moscow *soviet*, 250 in Kharkov, 120 in Yaroslav, 78 in Kremenchung and plenty of others in towns all over the country. The democracy of the new society was part of its self-discipline.

Perhaps the most extraordinary feature of the early years of the Russian revolution was the dedication of the working people to the running of their new society. In modern capitalist times rich and powerful people who have never made a sacrifice in their lives go on television to implore the majority, who spend in a week what their implorers spend on a single lunch, to make sacrifices for the 'national good'. Their country, it is said, depends on them working harder and accepting less. Few workers take this seriously, since there is no sign that the people who ask for the sacrifice plan to share in it. But in Russia in 1918, 1919 and 1920 working people not only saw that everyone was taking part in the sacrifice, but felt it was their society which benefited from it.

The liberal British journalist Arthur Ransome, later to become rich and famous from writing children's books, travelled widely in post-revolutionary Russia and reported in wonder for his paper **The Daily News**. His two books about Russia are full of admiration for the new society and the dedication to it of its working people.

He described an evening after a conference in Jaroslavl when he and Radek, a Bolshevik leader, were invited to see a play put on by railwaymen and their families. After the play, the workers called on Radek to make a speech:

> He led off by a direct and furious assault on the railway workers in general, demanding work, work and more work, telling them that as the Red Army had been the vanguard of the revolution hitherto... so now it was the turn of the railway workers. ... Instead of giving them a pleasant, interesting sketch of the international position, which, no doubt, was what they expected, he took the opportunity to tell them exactly how things stood at home. And the amazing thing was that they seemed to be pleased. They listened with extreme attention, wanted to turn out someone who had a sneezing fit at the far end of the hall, and nearly lifted the roof off with cheering when Radek had done. I wondered what sort of reception a man would have who in another country interrupted a play to hammer home truths about the need of work to an audience of working people who had gathered solely for the purpose of legitimate recreation.

Shortly before he left Russia, Arthur Ransome had an interview with Lenin. He asked him a shrewd question:

> 'Did he think they would pull through far enough economically to be able to satisfy the needs of the peasantry before that same peasantry had organised a real political opposition that should overwhelm them?' Lenin laughed: 'If I could answer that question,' he said, 'I could answer everything, for on the answer to that question everything depends. I think we can. Yes, I think we can. But I do not know that we can.'

The prospect that the socialist revolution could be overwhelmed by opposition from the peasantry had been faced squarely by Lenin and the Bolsheviks from the beginning of the revolution. They realised that they could not possibly sustain a socialist democracy for long within the bounds of a country the mass of whose population were peasants. The peasants had joined the revolution enthusiastically. It gave them the chance to seize the land from rapacious landlords and Tsarist plutocrats. But the peasants were not interested in a socialist society based on cooperation and democracy. They wanted land for themselves, which they could develop individually.

Two revolutions had therefore happened at the same time: in the cities for a socialist democracy; in the countryside for small ownership of land. Almost at once, as Lenin foresaw, the two revolutions started to work against one another. Since the working class was a small minority of the Russian population, the socialist democracy, if it was confined to Russia, was doomed.

Lenin spelt this out at a teachers' conference in May 1919:

> Even before the revolution, and likewise after it, our thought was: immediately, or at any rate very quickly, a revolution will begin in other countries, in capitalistically more developed countries—or in the contrary case, we will have to perish.

The whole of his strategy therefore was to use the revolution as an inspiration and agitation for revolutions in other 'more developed countries'—in particular Germany. If such revolutions did not break out and breathe life and sustenance into the tiny Russian working class, the alternative was simple and inevitable: 'we will have to perish'. Thus Lenin's foreign policy was directed to spreading revolution to other countries. The formation of new Communist parties was encouraged in Germany, France, Britain, Italy and elsewhere. The war had been ended on exceedingly unfavourable terms to Russia. Everything depended on the spark of revolution which had been struck in urban Russia igniting a revolutionary bonfire in Europe.

It did not happen. The German revolution, which broke out at the end of the war in 1918, was finally defeated in 1923. In Britain and France the workers preferred to stick to the parliamentary road. In Italy, the mass occupations of the factories in 1920 were defeated by the employers, who resorted soon after (as the German employers did a decade later) to fascism.

The Russian revolution was isolated. The working class which had made the revolution was almost entirely wiped out by war and famine. Of the three million adult workers in Russia, only 1.2 million remained in 1921, and many of those were driven out of the cities in search of food. Effectively the only revolutionary workers who were left were those who had taken over the reins of political power. The Bolsheviks still ruled, but there were no Bolshevik workers to maintain 'control from below'—the essence of the revolution. The inevitable happened quite quickly. The revolution perished.

No one can tell the exact moment when day becomes night, but everyone can tell the difference between light and darkness. Many socialists over the past 70 years have refused to accept that the Russian revolution was lost because there was no one moment, no cataclysmic upheaval in which the forces of reaction staged a counter-revolution and overthrew the Russian revolutionary government. This is strictly true. There was no moment of truth when the revolutionary bull was slain. Slain he was, however. The system of society in Russia in the 1930s was quite different from that thrown up by the Russian revolution.

Lenin died in 1924—not long after the defeat of the German revolution. By that time a different political animal was filling the ranks of the Communist Party. These people were not inspired by the self-emancipation of 1917. They listened appreciatively to the views and priorities of the general secretary of the Communist Party, Stalin, against whose intolerance Lenin had warned in his will. Stalin and his supporters had no time for the 'luxuries' of opposition (which had been tolerated and put to good effect when there were many fewer luxuries about).

Stalin insisted on the mummification of Lenin's body and the deification of Lenin's name. This was a grotesque flouting of everything Lenin had ever stood for—he had resisted to his dying day the slightest sign of reverence for any God or for any human being, particularly himself. The plans for his mummification were bitterly opposed by Lenin's wife and by those who knew and loved him. But they suited the purpose of the General Secretary.

Before long, with the support of the new workers in the factories, and of the rapidly-growing political police, Stalin was 'purging' the party of all opposition. Leon Trotsky, a leader of the

Russian revolution second in stature only to Lenin himself, was hounded and abused. In 1927, he was exiled. His exile paved the way for a complete reversal of the economic priorities of the revolution.

Most of the economic effort immediately after the revolution had been devoted to driving out the counter-revolutionary armies. But no one doubted that the central thrust of economic activity in the new society was to make a better world for the workers and the dispossessed. The object of investment, for instance, was to produce consumer goods that would improve workers' lives. In 1928, in spite of all the dreadful privations suffered by the Russian revolution, 60.5 per cent of the goods produced were 'consumer' goods.

Stalin's Five-Year Plans, which started in 1928, changed all that completely. The first two plans almost exactly halved the percentage of production devoted to consumer goods. The priority was accumulation, reinvesting wealth in further production. The more Russian workers produced, and production rose hugely, the less they got for their own needs, and the more went on industrial investment, on tanks and bombs, on more, still more, industrial investment, and on privileges for the new bureaucracy.

One by one the gains of the revolution were cast aside. Women's liberation, for instance, was a menace to the regimented society which was necessary to fulfil the new norms. Out went the decree on free divorce, out went the decree on free abortion; in came the Great Russian family, and even the Great Russian Orthodox Church.

The worst impediment to the new Stalinist aims, however, was the Russian revolution itself. In words the revolution had to be honoured, just as the French revolution is still verbally honoured by a Parisian establishment that is anything but revolutionary. But the reality of the revolution, and particularly of the ruling Communist Party which was riddled with revolutionaries, was a menace to Stalin and his followers. For ten years and more they conducted their war on the revolutionaries with a single-minded savagery which was borrowed, often literally, from the barbaric regime of Ivan the Terrible.

Stalin's hatred of opposition was maniacal. The Italian socialist Ignazio Silone described a meeting of the executive of the Communist International in Moscow in May 1927. Silone led the Communist underground in Italy, which was fighting a brutal fascist government. He and his fellow Italian delegate, Togliatti, were late for the meeting. When they arrived, the chairman, Thälmann, leader of the German Communist Party, was reading out an hysterical denunciation of a paper by Trotsky criticising the recent Russian policy in China—which had led to the mass slaughter of Chinese Communists.

Silone apologised for arriving late and for not having seen the document which was being condemned. 'To tell the truth,' said Thälmann, 'we haven't seen the document either.' Refusing to believe what he had heard, Silone blamed the interpreter. He repeated that he could not possibly pass judgement on something he had not read. Stalin, standing by the window, said softly that if the resolution was not unanimous it could not be submitted.

Tremendous pressure was brought on the Italian delegates that evening and the following day to reconsider their position —which to their credit they refused to do. They were denounced as 'petit bourgeois'—and Thälmann remarked that there was little wonder fascism had taken root in Italy if the Italian Communists were capable of such indiscipline.

Already, in 1927, the new rulers of Stalinist Russia were turning with increasing frenzy on every manifestation of the revolutionary tradition. Soon after leaving that meeting of the International, Ignazio Silone was approached by an Italian Communist who had escaped to Russia to avoid fascist persecution. He was proud to have been taken on by a Russian factory. Wrote Silone:

> He was ready to put up with the material shortages of every kind since to remedy them was clearly beyond the power of individuals, but he could not understand why the workers were entirely at the mercy of the factory directorate and had no effective organisation to protect their interests; why, in this respect also, they should be so much worse off than in capitalist countries. Most of the much-vaunted rights of the working class were purely theoretical.

There were still hundreds of thousands of workers who asked such questions in Russia in 1927. The new Stalinist regime bent every muscle to wipe them off the face of the earth. Anyone who breathed a word of socialism from below, even if they demanded the most marginal representation in the workplace, were shipped off to labour camps, or executed.

This persecution of the revolutionaries went on throughout the 1930s. By the end of that decade there was only one member of the original central committee of the Communist Party still living: Stalin himself. Lenin had died of illness. Every other member had been executed, murdered or forced into suicide. Most of the Bolshevik leaders were executed after show trials, in which they were either tortured or persuaded to 'confess' to their opposition to the revolution they had led. Bukharin, Zinoviev, Kamenev, Radek —all confessed and were shot. Trotsky was pursued into exile and murdered by a Stalinist agent in Mexico.

The whole disgusting process was brilliantly satirised by the British socialist writer George Orwell in his famous fable **Animal Farm**. The ultimate horror of the story was the dispatching of the old warhorse Boxer, strong, loyal and revolutionary to the last muscle, to the knacker's yard.

George Orwell was an exception among socialist writers in the rest of the world. Some of his most famous books—including **Animal Farm**—were rejected by publishers who detested Orwell for his opposition to Stalinist Russia. The enormous majority of socialists all over the world felt it was their duty to stand up for Stalinist Russia against its capitalist detractors. Some were prepared to support any monstrosity provided it emerged from the 'socialist motherland'. Others felt uneasy about, say, the show trials of the late 1930s, but were prepared to defend Russia as the 'lesser evil'.

Almost unanimously they accepted the definition of Russia as 'socialist'. They referred to the fact that there was no stock exchange, no shareholders robbing the workers of the value of what they produced. They insisted that the Russian economy was planned. Socialism, they argued, was a planned economy with no private enterprise, no individual shareholding in the means of production. This existed in Russia, therefore Russia was a socialist country. For nearly 30 years, through the Second World War and on beyond Stalin's death in 1953, the most courageous and militant socialists everywhere on earth stood shoulder to shoulder with one of the most reactionary dictatorships ever known.

How could this happen? Precisely because the definition of

socialism which hypnotised the left did not include its most essential ingredient: workers' control. An economic plan on its own, after all, could not be enough to define a socialist society. The crucial question is: what is the plan for?

The Russian plans under Stalin (and since) served no other purpose except to build up the Russian economy to compete with other economies. For this purpose the workers were directly excluded from decisions. The control of society was from above, not from below. It was, as it sometimes even called itself, a command economy. The commanders were appointed from above, not from below. They were the *nomenklatura*, leading party and state officials who were carefully selected and who performed the functions (and accepted the privileges) of a ruling class. They organised production to accumulate the national wealth at the expense of the Russian workers—exactly the function of the ruling class in every other country of the world. It mattered not a damn what forms this exploitation took, nor whether the Russian rulers rewarded themselves with shareholdings or with hunting lodges, travel permits, high salaries or servants. It was exploitation none the less.

Russia was not a socialist society at all. It was a state-capitalist society presided over by a tyranny every bit as savage as any stock exchange-based capitalist tyranny anywhere else in the world.

The support socialists in other countries gave to Stalinist Russia turned them into the unwitting tools of Russian foreign policy, which was as manipulative and cynical as any other foreign policy. In the early 1930s the menace of fascism, which had already taken power in Italy, started to threaten the whole of Central Europe. In Germany the left was split, almost evenly, between the Communists and the Social Democrats. A united left would have had the strike power, the influence in the communities and even the votes to beat off Hitler's Nazis. The crisis called out for a campaign by the Communists to put pressure on the Social Democratic leaders to unite with them against Hitler. But because of Stalin's reckless foreign policy, the German Communist Party turned its main fire not on the Nazis but on the Social Democrats, who it described as 'social fascists'. The campaign irrevocably split the working-class movement, and Hitler was able to seize power. After that the Social Democrats and the Communists were united at last: in the concentration camps and the gas chambers.

The debilitating disease of Stalinism is expertly described by the novelist Doris Lessing in her 1962 masterpiece, **The Golden Notebook**. One of her characters, a Communist Party loyalist, goes to Russia, and returns with a story. He had, he said, been sitting in his hotel when he got a call from the Kremlin. Comrade Stalin would like to see him. All excited, he had been rushed to The Presence. An ordinary man in ordinary clothes, with a neat moustache and smoking a pipe, had asked for an account of developments in the British labour movement. The visitor, overcome with gratitude, blurted out what he could. Kindly and sympathetically Comrade Stalin offered a few words of advice, and begged to be allowed to get on with his work. Doris Lessing records, and she is certainly right, that every single Communist visitor to Russia in the two decades of the 1930s and 1940s suffered from the same fantasy.

The tragedy of it all is that the socialism which all those people represented, their fighting spirit, was dragged back to a crass utopianism in which the soul of socialism, the activity and control of the self-emancipated working class, was at worst replaced, at best personified, by a pipe-smoking despot.

Some socialists, like Ignazio Silone and Doris Lessing, were so repulsed by Stalinism that they left the Communist Party, and moved off to the right (Silone became a right-wing Social Democrat, and Doris Lessing's novels, which had started with such zest and hope, degenerated into mystical reaction).

The first great shock for the mass of Communist Party members came three years after Stalin's death when his successor, Khrushchev, denounced some of the horrors of the Stalinist period. Some Communists fled to the right or to apathy; some—a very few—to other socialist organisations. But the Communist parties survived the Khrushchev outburst, even when Khrushchev was chucked out and replaced by a regime which differed only on the margins from Stalin's.

By the 1970s, the central claim with which socialists and Communists had defended their support for 'socialism from above' in Russia began to wear thin. Whatever else could be said about Stalinist Russia, they had argued, its economic growth was spectacular. Between 1928 and 1968, the Russian economy had doubled and redoubled. The puny working class of 1920, only a million strong, had been transformed into an industrial working class of more than sixty million. Russia could mount an army to defeat Hitler's at Stalingrad and launch a Sputnik into space before even the United States of America.

All this had been achieved by a 'command economy', by state capitalism. But state capitalism has its limitations as well. It is an excellent system for bludgeoning a peasant society into mass industrial production. But it suffers from its own success. It can order production, bully and command workers to achieve higher and higher norms in heavy industries. But when it has to deal with more advanced technologies, to persuade and absorb skilled labour, to distribute goods as well as to produce them, state capitalism flounders.

The Russian economy has been floundering for a long time. For twenty years this 'socialist country' has been importing grain from its allegedly more inefficient capitalist rival, the United States of America. Economic growth rates have been much lower in the 1970s and 1980s than in the 1930s and 1940s. The argument that its planned economy would always provide Russia with a faster growth rate than its capitalist rivals has been confounded. On almost every front in the past fifteen years or so the Russian economy has been eclipsed by that of America. By comparison with the even more spectacular growth rates in Germany and Japan, Russia has been left far behind.

It is this failure of the central argument for a state-capitalist economy which has caused all the 'rethink' and 'reform' in Russia in recent years. If Russian state capitalism was to compete successfully with the West, then it would have to relax its central controls and open up to the world market. The 'command' economy had to be supplanted by a 'demand' economy. Workers had to be lured and incorporated rather than bullied. The privileges of the bureaucrat had to be replaced with the privileges of the entrepreneur.

This could be achieved only with a violent shake-up in the crumbling, corrupt Russian bureaucracy. If *perestroika* (economic reforms designed to make Russia more competitive) was to succeed, a little *glasnost* (free discussion and debate) was called for.

The man who started to put these anti-bureaucratic principles into practice was a bureaucrat who had himself climbed steadily up the Communist Party ladder without at any time appearing to oppose the reactionaries Brezhnev, Andropov or Chernenko. Mikhail Gorbachev had done nothing in particular, but he had done it very well. He had a forthright attractive manner, understood the importance of public relations, and he dressed well.

At once, the massed ranks of former Stalinists all over the world fell in love with this new anti-Stalinist reformer. The romantic attachment many of them had with Russia as a 'socialist country' was brought to life in the personality of this 'bustling man of peace'. Here was a man who really would put 'socialist Russia' on the world agenda, who did not execute people who disagreed with him, and who would almost single-handedly bring about 'revolution from above'.

Years of looking upwards had craned their necks and stunted their vision. If for a moment they had shifted their gaze downwards to the heaving, struggling working class of Russia they would have seen profound discontent, exploitation, squalor, hunger and a seething anger. All these got worse as Gorbachev and the 'reformers' tried to apply the standards of multinational corporations to state-capitalist corporations. In this much-heralded change, there was nothing to be gained by the Russian workers. Indeed, if anything, the market 'medicine' was even worse for the workers than the state-capitalist disease.

The vast Russian working class began to fight. In 1989, the coalfields of Siberia and the Ukraine, for the first time since the revolution, were paralysed by strikes. Gorbachev told the Supreme Soviet:

> This is perhaps the worst ordeal to befall our country in all four years of restructuring. There has been Chernobyl, there have been various other misfortunes. Nevertheless, I am singling this out as the most serious and difficult.

It was bad enough trying to oust the incompetent and corrupt officials who made up the Russian state-capitalist machine. They would fight tooth and nail for their privileges, exposing and denouncing their fellow bureaucrats in the process. But the prospect of facing down the huge Russian working class, at last galvanised into action, and even, horror of horrors, reading and listening to arguments about socialism from below, was much more serious.

Gorbachev backed off, allowing the miners the luxury of a

little soap, and holding back a little from the excesses of *perestroika*. For most of 1989 and all of 1990 this Gorbachev, who came before the world in 1985 and 1986 as a determined and confident reformer, spent his time retracing his steps, then gingerly stepping out again. No sooner had he carried out an economic reform here, than he refused to carry out one somewhere else. No sooner had he sided with the 'reformers' in the Supreme Soviet than he denounced them. All his political life and experience has been 'from above' and he intends to keep things there. Grafting private enterprise capitalism on to state capitalism is a difficult business, and Gorbachev intends to do it by keeping the class which he represents in economic power—whatever deprivation that may cause the rest.

Russian workers and reformers who adored him in 1985 and 1986 now detest him. Utterly confused by the mirage of reform, contradicted at every turn by reality, the world's Communist parties have vanished in the wind like a puff of smoke. Sixty years of mythology about a socialist motherland are exposed for all to see.

What is left is something much more substantial: the working class of Russia in motion, and the working class of Eastern Europe, which in six fantastic months in 1989 helped to overthrow six state capitalist tyrannies masquerading as socialism from above, have started to pave the way to a completely different future: socialism from below.

3: THE TOTTERING THRONES

'All [that has happened]... is only a beginning. The system that impedes the liberation of man in our country can only be negated by actions, not words; a revolutionary disavowal—the only authentic sort—cannot be attained by a pure and simple substitution of persons. Otherwise the tottering thrones will remain thrones from which a new oligarchic bureaucracy will exercise control over us all.'

—K Bartosek, 'Open letter to the Czechoslovak workers', 1968.

WHAT WAS commonly known as socialism came to the countries of Eastern Europe not from any action of the working people there, but on the back of an envelope.

While discussing the spoils for the victors of the Second World War, Winston Churchill, prime minister of Britain, jotted down some suggestions for Stalin, dictator of Russia, as to what should happen in Eastern Europe. The basis of Churchill's plan was that the Russians could do what they liked in Bulgaria, Romania and Hungary provided they left Britain to 'deal with' the Communists in Greece.

Stalin was delighted with this plan, which he vigorously ticked, urging Churchill to keep the envelope as a memento of their grand diplomacy. Stalin already had control of East Germany and Poland, whose capital, Warsaw, had been almost totally destroyed by the Nazis while Russian troops stood by. He was soon to get control of Czechoslovakia too. Without further ado, he and his armies set about establishing 'socialism' in his six new satellites, whose combined population was about a hundred million. His method for bringing this 'socialism' about was exactly the same as it had been in Russia: brute force.

If there was any romantic among the Eastern European working class who imagined that the long night of Nazi occupation was now to end in a socialist dawn, he or she was soon to be disillusioned. In Bulgaria in 1944, for instance, the liberated workers set up their own councils, elected tribunals to arrest and try fascists, and disbanded the police force. All this horrified and incensed the Russian foreign secretary Molotov, who issued a declaration after meeting a Bulgarian government delegation:

> If certain Communists continue their present conduct, we will bring them to reason. Bulgaria will remain with her democratic government and her present order... You must retain all valuable army officers from before the *coup d'état*. You should reinstate in service all officers who have been dismissed for various reasons.

The Bulgarian Army had been behaving with some jubilation in liberated areas such as Thrace and Macedonia, and had even elected workers' councils and hoisted red flags instead of their regimental emblems. This was the subject of a stern rebuke from the new minister of war, who had strong support in Moscow. His order was: 'to return at once to normal discipline, to abolish soldiers' councils and to hoist no more red flags.'

Once these initial enthusiasms had been doused, the Russian authorities set about transforming the poverty-stricken and rural countries into industrial economies. They started by setting up their stooges in coalition governments which included politicians who had supported the Nazi occupations.

In Romania for instance the minister of culture in the March 1945 government, set up with Stalin's support, was Mihail Raila, a fervent admirer of Hitler. At least four other ministers had been supporters of the fascist Iron Guard, which had welcomed the Nazi army of occupation. The man who had commanded the Romanian troops who fought against the Russians at Stalingrad was now promoted and made assistant chief of staff.

Even before they were able to get the Eastern European governments entirely under their thumb, the Russians made sure of their control of the army and the security services. In East Germany, they inherited Hitler's intelligence service—and maintained it almost without changes. In Hungary, the Communist Party set up the State Security Authority and in the words of the hard-line Stalinist Hungarian leader Rakosi: 'We kept this organisation in our hands from the first day of its establishment.'

After seizing and adopting the state machine which had persecuted the workers under the Nazis, the Stalinists set about seizing hold of the governments. There were two immediate problems.

First, the Communist parties were too small even to pretend to command mass support. The Romanian Communist Party in mid-1944 had only 1000 members. A year and a quarter later, this had grown to a fantastic 800,000. The Polish Communist Party had 30,000 members in January 1945—and 300,000 in April. In Czechoslovakia, a party of 27,000 grew by the beginning of 1946 to a mass organisation of 1,159,164 members. Were these all workers voluntarily flocking to the red flags of the revolution? They were not. The new recruits (unlike the old members) were the élite of society, the upwardly mobile minority which yearned for advancement and for privilege, and who felt that the state-capitalist programme of the Communist Party was the only way to get their country—and themselves—out of the rut.

The second problem was that in some countries there were vibrant social-democratic parties which had a far better claim to represent the workers than had the Communist parties. In Poland and in Hungary, the Socialist Party was stronger than the Communist Party. In both cases this was dealt with by a forcible merger. In Poland 82,000 members of the Socialist Party were expelled for objecting. One of them, the secretary of the Polish trade unions, Adam Kurylowicz, wrote a pamphlet accusing the Polish Communist Party of conducting a reign of terror in the factories:

> They fire and hire workers without taking into account the opinion of the workers of the plant, scorning the laws, conquests and social rights of the workers. A clique of self-seeking politicians is being formed. These new dignitaries have discovered that a party book is more important than technical qualifications.

Adam Kurylowicz had discovered early what the entire working class of Eastern Europe were to find to their cost over the next 44 years: that the Russian government was creating in all six countries a bureaucracy after its own image: a bureaucracy which was to play the part of a ruling class.

Exactly the same methods which had been used by Stalin and his henchmen in Russia were used by his satellite bureaucracies in Eastern Europe. Every breath of democracy was squeezed out. Workers' committees which had been set up after the war in some countries, such as Czechoslovakia, were quickly disbanded and replaced by one-man management. The most ruthless discipline was imposed on the workers. At least half a million 'troublesome' East European workers were consigned to slave labour camps.

No politician, especially if he had become a Communist under the influence of the Russian revolution, was safe from Stalin's periodic purges. In the most savage of these, the general secretary of the Czech party, Slansky, and several leading party figures were condemned to death after confessing to anti-party crimes in exactly the same hideous and inquisitorial ceremony laid down by the Moscow show trials of the 1930s. The Communist veterans who had fought in the underground were effectively wiped out. By 1953, only 1.5 per cent of the members of the Communist Party of Czechoslovakia had held party cards before the war. It had been, per head of the population, by far the largest in Eastern Europe.

The internationalism that had inspired the revolutionary Communists after 1917 was replaced by a wild and hysterical nationalism. All the superstitions and vendettas which had cut swathes of blood through Eastern Europe from the Middle Ages were revived. The Germans in the Sudetenland, in Czechoslovakia, a peaceful and essentially social-democratic people, were rounded up in a series of pogroms organised by the new Communist government. The Communist minister for education, whose party took its name from the works of Karl Marx and Frederick Engels (both of them German), declared on 29 March 1945: 'We do not know any progressive Germans, nor are there any.'

In the same way, Czech was set against Hungarian, and Hungarian against Romanian. No chauvinist or racist claptrap was out of bounds for these new 'communist' rulers.

All sorts of obstacles stood in the way of economic growth for the state-capitalist satellites of Russia. Russia had looted them all: 84 per cent of one year's entire production in Romania was seized in 'war reparations'. Looting by 'reparation' was followed by looting by trade. The terms of trade were fixed across the board so that the satellites sold cheap to Russia, and bought dear.

Nevertheless, roughly the same pattern of state-capitalist development in Russia was followed in its satellites. The economies, run by force and fear, grew. Backward peasant countries became industrial powers. Poland, for instance, an overwhelmingly agricultural country before the war, became by the 1970s the world's tenth industrial power (with the eighth highest military budget). In all six countries, only 14 per cent of the working population had been wage earners before the war. By 1980, this had jumped to 60 per cent. In the early years of the East European state capitalisms, growth rates were faster or as fast as anywhere in Western Europe.

As with Russia, however, after the initial burst of economic growth, state capitalism started to lose its dynamism. Wild fluctuations in the growth rates sometimes even of different industries led to a growing wrath among the workers—who now added economic discontent to their anger at disenfranchisement and bullying. Even more than in Russia, and much quicker, this resentment gave way to open revolt.

In East Germany in June 1953 a demonstration of building workers against impossible new norms flared into a mass working-class revolt. The revolt was suppressed by the bullets of 25,000 hastily convened Russian troops. Only after the revolt did the propagandists of Western capitalism suggest that it had been inspired by pro-Western aims. During the revolt the West German government kept its distance and warned its people against taking part in any 'dangerous actions'. The East German rising was led by old Communists, people who had fought against Hitler's fascism. After the revolt, tens of thousands of them were purged from the ruling East German Communist Party.

In Hungary in 1956, a students' demonstration called in solidarity with striking workers and dissident intellectuals in Poland quickly blossomed into a full-scale revolution. Almost at once a new form of power rose again, apparently from nothing, to haunt the Hungarian rulers and their Russian masters. Workers' councils were set up in workplaces and revolutionary councils were elected by area. These became the administrative power, far stronger, fairer and more representative than the government. Peter Fryer was the correspondent in Hungary for the British Communist Party paper, **The Daily Worker**. He reported on the revolutionary council at Gyor:

> In their spontaneous origin, in their composition, in their sense of responsibility, in their efficient organisation of food supplies and civil order, in the restraint they exercised on the wild elements among the youth, in the wisdom with which so many of them handled the problem of Soviet troops, and, not least, in their striking resemblance to the workers', peasants' and soldiers' councils which sprang up in Russia in the 1905 revolution and in February 1917, these committees, a network of which now extended over the whole of Hungary, were remarkably uniform. They were at once organs of insurrection—the coming together of delegates elected by factories and universities, mines and army units—and organs of popular self-government which the armed people trusted... The revolution thrust them forward, aroused their civic pride and latent genius for organisation, set them to work to build democracy out of the ruins of democracy.

Here was the spectre of 'socialism from below' of 1905 and 1917, which scared the 'reformist' Russian leaders under Khrushchev every bit as much as it had scared Stalin in the old days. The Russian government acted in the only way it knew. The Hungarian revolution was crushed by an enormous expeditionary force led by Russian tanks. The revolutionary councils were able to resist the troops for several days with a magnificent and utterly solid general strike.

For a moment socialism lived and breathed—and demonstrated to the world that the power and capacity of the working class was something wholly different and implacably opposed to the state-capitalist tyranny which, in the name of socialism, took socialism by the throat and throttled it.

The next country to revolt was the jewel in the crown of Russia's empire: Czechoslovakia. A small country, with its relatively large working class and developed industries, it had prospered during the first years of state-capitalist rule. By the early 1960s, however, the growth suddenly and unexpectedly staggered to a halt. In 1963 production actually went down. The economic crisis led to a collapse of confidence in the ruling Communist Party. Journalists and intellectuals began to say what they thought, and to challenge the Stalinist orthodoxy. Some were locked up and persecuted, but the pressure continued. In 1967 the Stalinist dinosaur Novotny was replaced as general secretary of the Czech Communist Party by a little-known Slovak called Alexander Dubcek.

There followed the 'Prague spring' in which for a brief moment the hopes of the whole Czech people fluttered. A group of intellectuals wrote a manifesto for a new dawn: **2000 Words**. Commentators believed then and believe now that Dubcek put himself at the head of this movement, and represented its aspirations. In fact Dubcek, like Khrushchev before him and Gorbachev after him, was a party man, bred in the party machine. He swam with the tide because it was unstoppable—except, once again, by Russian troops.

After the huge Russian invasion of August 1968, the middle-class opposition dwindled, to be replaced by a series of mass strikes in the factories, and the election of workers' councils. These councils did not take power, as they had done in Hungary. They acted rather as expressions of the people's demands against government, which, for nearly a year after the invasion, still included Dubcek. There were some who recognised the weakness of the councils, and of the protest movement generally. Writing in the dissident weekly **Reporter**, K Bartosek was one:

> The act which can begin to change your condition is the election and activity of organs of workers' self-management, in which together, by yourselves, you administer what belongs to you... Without democracy in the factories, one cannot speak of a democratic society.

Though councils were elected, and though for months they remained the only real opposition to the new Russian stooge government, they were not organs of power, and they withered away in the reaction which followed Dubcek's removal and the gradual return to state-capitalist rule.

The workers' councils were to appear again, in a different form, in the last of the great explosions which racked state-capitalist

Eastern Europe before the storm of 1989. In Poland, the authorities were in almost continual trouble with a hungry and angry people. In 1956 and 1970 there had been widespread food riots, demonstrations and strikes in protest against the price of food. It was the price of meat in particular which set off the strike, in 1980, that led to the formation of the mass trade union Solidarity.

In most developed countries of the West, trade unions had become what they were after a long, careful and cautious development. After the mass strike of the summer of 1980 in Poland, a single trade union, unfettered by craft or demarcation, was joined by ten million workers: 80 per cent of the entire Polish workforce. This was a higher level of trade union organisation than in any other country in the world.

The secret of this astonishing success was the form of organisation developed by the workers in their struggle. It was called, clumsily, the Inter-Enterprise Strike Committee. It was yet another manifestation of the *soviet*, the workers' council, the workers' committee which had been so prominent in Russia in 1917, in Hungary in 1956, in Czechoslovakia in 1968, and for that matter in Portugal in 1974 and 1975, when its fascist regime, forty years old, was finally cast aside.

The same characteristics were immediately in evidence; the courage in fighting for economic and political demands; the responsibility and discipline in their own ranks (booze was confiscated outside the gates of the striking factories and the bottles destroyed); above all the seeds of the new society blossoming in the struggle against the old one. Solidarity represented exactly what it called itself: cooperation, equality, concern for the disadvantaged, contempt for the exploiters. It created again, as part of its struggle to come into existence, the institutions which could run a quite different society—a socialist society. It too was inspired by the spirit of socialism, self-emancipation and workers' democracy.

Ranged against it was a regime which was socialist only in name, and anti-socialist in everything else. One of the two opposing forces had to smash the other—or be broken. Because Solidarity never saw itself as more than a trade union, an organisation bargaining with the powers-that-be, it never struck the decisive blow. When the axe did fall, it was wielded by the Polish regime, with the full force of Moscow's support behind it. Just before Christmas

1981, in a series of carefully-planned raids by the secret police, Solidarity was broken, its leaders arrested, its committees disbanded. All the hopes which it had held out for the oppressed people of Poland seemed to be drowned forever.

With the Polish revolt crushed, the regimes of Eastern Europe settled down for a brief moment into the old groove. They were still described by loyal, if weary, Communists all over the world as 'socialist countries'.

Other more sophisticated socialists sought other descriptions. They called them 'degenerated workers' states' or simply 'bureaucratic regimes' which defied any definition by class. In truth, however, the central characteristic of those at the top of these societies was that they were ruling classes, exploiting the workers and the peasants, and sliding into greater and greater chaos and corruption.

In Romania, the regime of Nicolai Ceausescu was briefly feted in the West because, allegedly, it challenged its Russian masters. Yet the Ceausescu regime had become a caricature of an exploiting tyranny. Ceausescu bent all his energies to storing up more wealth for himself, his family and his associates out of the surplus his government and secret police wrenched from the already impoverished Romanian workers and peasants. On his command, 80,000 people were forcibly moved from their homes to make way for the most grotesque and luxurious palace in all Europe. And this was merely the dictator's second home! He selected from orphanages the cream of his secret police so that they could regard him and his wife as their Father and Mother. He sprayed them with privileges of every kind—the secret police were even better fed and clothed than the captains of industry. He published phoney statistics suggesting the economy was permanently growing and even rigged the weather reports. Workers' resistance—such as the miners' strikes in the early 1980s—was put down with the most appalling repression.

What Ceausescu did in Romania was only a more monstrous replica of what Honecker was doing in East Germany, Husak in Czechoslovakia or Zhikov in Bulgaria. Yet somehow socialists everywhere, duped by the old formulas of public ownership and 'planning', continued to pretend that these regimes were in some way 'better' or 'more working-class' than the regimes of the West.

The argument cut little ice with the oppressed people of Eastern Europe. On the contrary, as the repression and corruption grew, so the very notion of socialism, so repeatedly ascribed to the regimes themselves, became anathema.

At the top of society the ruling classes, forced more and more to trade and compete with Western capitalist countries, developed a theory of 'market socialism'. They talked about a 'socialist' society where economic decisions were made by the market. As the absurdity of a socialist system directed by the market became more and more obvious, the word 'socialism' was discreetly dropped from the formula. 'Market socialism' became 'market'. The ruling classes of the East yearned for the 'simple disciplines' of market capitalism. They longed for the day when the restrictions of state capitalism could be shuffled off, and replaced by untramelled free enterprise.

For most of the 1980s, however, the ruling classes of Eastern Europe played ball with state capitalism. Down below, however, where people were more prepared to make personal sacrifices, the revolt simmered, then boiled over.

But here too there was now an important change. In every previous uprising in Eastern Europe since the war—East Germany in 1953, Hungary in 1956, Poland in 1956, 1970 and 1980—the intellectuals, students and workers who took part had demanded some form of socialism. No one ever suggested that they wanted to return to the capitalist society which existed in the West. As the repression and corruption dragged on, however, and as the state capitalist societies found it more and more difficult to fulfil even the most basic workers' needs, the demands and aspirations changed. People in East Germany looked across the border to West Germany and saw a more prosperous society. They envied free elections, a free press, freedom to demonstrate and challenge governments—all of which seemed to exist in the West.

Socialism fell off the agenda. Even the most committed socialists in the eastern bloc, many of them exhausted by long prison sentences, dropped their vision of a new sort of socialism and settled instead for a change from state capitalism to multinational capitalism. They were content for their detested regimes to be replaced by elected parliaments, which would preside over free-enterprise capitalism as they did in the West. All talk of revolution, and therefore of workers' councils, *soviets*, revolutionary committees, seemed at best out of date, at worst representative of a long and wearisome struggle against forces which seemed invincible.

When the storm broke, it broke suddenly and overwhelmingly. In a matter of months the rulers of Eastern Europe followed each other into oblivion, just as the kings, emperors and kaisers had done in the months which followed the First World War.

The collapse started in Poland, where, under pressure of more strikes and an intractable economic crisis, the same General Jaruzelski who had led the repression of Solidarity in 1981 now summoned Solidarity to join the government of Poland. Half-free elections returned a Solidarity government under the presidency of... General Jaruzelski.

But the signal had gone out and it stirred the masses all over Eastern Europe into action. Mass demonstrations, occasionally supported by strikes, toppled the rulers one by one: Honecker in East Germany; Husak in Czechoslovakia. Kadar in Hungary and Zhikov in Bulgaria were removed more discreetly. These regimes contemplated resisting the masses by brute force, but this time there were no Russian troops on hand to prop them up. All these governments were toppled with hardly a struggle. Only in Romania did the dictator Ceausescu lash out in the only way he knew. His secret police rallied to his call to put down demonstrations and fired into crowds at Timosoara. But before long the Romanian army had sized up the balance of forces, and turned against him. Like so many dictators before him, he suddenly found that no one, not even his bodyguard, was on his side.

The governments had gone, and elections were held, often returning conservative or liberal administrations. The heads of industrial enterprises, the generals, the judges, the senior civil servants, even most of the police and intelligence chiefs remained in office. The politicians, too, who now sought votes from the people, were by and large the old bureaucrats who now declared that they had 'reformed'. One East German party leader had hastily to resign in the middle of the elections when he was exposed as a former leader of the hated Stasi—the secret police. Others, with equally delicate pasts, managed to cover up history with bold declarations of their faith in the 'new democracy'.

The actions of the people, the mass demonstrations and where necessary the strikes, had toppled the old rulers. That was the first important lesson of the astonishing events of 1989. But the demonstrators would soon have cause to remember Bartosek's prophetic warning way back in 1968: that real change could not come about just by 'the substitution of persons'. The 'tottering thrones,' he had warned, 'would remain thrones from which a new oligarchic bureaucracy will exercise control over us all.' A host of advisers, entrepreneurs, capitalists, media proprietors and economists flooded into Eastern Europe to vindicate this prophecy. They brought a new message from the West. State capitalism, they insisted (correctly), was a failure. Private-enterprise capitalism, good old market multinational capitalism, works.

But does it ?

4: THE GROWING WRATH

'Men have transformed the world with their knowledge. The short lean wheat has been made big and productive. Little sour apples have grown large and sweet, and that old grape that grew among the trees and fed the big birds has mothered a thousand varieties, red and black, green and pale pink, purple and yellow; and each variety with its own flavour.

'The men who work in the experimental farms have made new fruits; nectarines and forty kinds of plums, walnuts with paper shells and always they work, selecting, grafting, changing, driving themselves, driving the earth to produce.

'But men who graft the trees and make the seeds fertile and big can find no way to make the hungry eat their produce.

'A million people hungry, needing the fruit—and kerosene spread over the golden mountains. And the smell of rot fills the country.

'The people come with nets to fish for potatoes in the river, and the guards hold them back. They come in rattling cars to get the dumped oranges but the kerosene is sprayed. And they stand still and watch the potatoes flow by, listen to the screaming pigs being killed in a ditch and covered with quicklime, watch the mountains of oranges slop down to a putrefying ooze.

'And in the eyes of the people there is a failure and in the eyes of the hungry there is a growing wrath.'

—*John Steinbeck,* **The Grapes of Wrath**.

RICH AND POWERFUL people are always explaining how they wish to expand their wealth and power not for themselves but for everyone else. Their basic claim for the 'free-market' system which has made them rich is that it is the only known system which fits what is produced to what people want and need.

Yet the plainest fact of all about a world dominated by the free market system demonstrates exactly the opposite. From every corner of the world comes the suffocated howl of millions of people whose desperate needs and wants are being systematically ignored.

'The poor,' Jesus Christ is reported as saying, 'ye have always with you.' We have them with us now in greater numbers than he or the Devil can ever have imagined. Thirty years ago the chairman of the Food and Agriculture Organisation of the United Nations warned that unless the 'rich nations' of the world substantially raised the proportion of their incomes in 'aid' to the 'developing countries', the chief beneficiaries would be the Four Horsemen of the Apocalypse.

The Four Horsemen—Famine, Disease, Ignorance and Death—have been riding roughshod over the world ever since. The World Bank estimated in 1988 that a billion people—one in five of the total world population—were living in 'absolute poverty' in conditions where the chief hope for any of them was survival beyond the age of five. The World Bank, as ever, underestimated the problem. A report on the decade of the 1980s from the Washington-based Worldwatch Institute put the figure at a higher 1.2 billion people, or 23.4 per cent of the world population.

In the 1980s, 'the decade of the free market', these numbers—and the proportion—rose for the first time for fifty years. In every previous decade since the end of the Second World War, the percentage of 'absolute poor' in the world had been marginally reduced. Now, in the decade of the system whose supreme quality is claimed to be the fitting of production to need, it has grown.

Most of the people in 43 countries (not including the two biggest countries on earth, China and India, where there were slight improvements) ended the 1980s worse off than at the start of the decade.

The chief casualties were children. In Peru, a third of all the children are stunted and deformed because they don't get enough to eat. Child deaths from hunger in Zambia doubled in the first half of the 1980s. In Brazil, more babies died in infancy in the mid-1980s than at any other time—the first such increase for twenty years.

In a desperate attempt to drive home the full horror of what is going on, the United Nations Children's Fund declared in its 1989 annual report:

> At least half a million young children have died in the last twelve months as a result of the slowing down or the reversal of progress in the developing world.

Even this was wrong, because huge tracts of the 'developing' world are not developing any longer. As a direct result of the genius of the market system, enormous sums of money have been lent to poor countries at high rates of interest. In 1989, the so-called developing world owed more than a trillion dollars—a million million—nearly half the value of everything they produced.

If the people of Zambia paid *everything* they produced to the bankers and investment companies who have loaned their country money, it would still take them three full years to pay off the interest charges. If they did that, of course (which they cannot), none of them would exist. As it is, many hundreds of thousands will perish anyway, while the rest try to scratch some kind of survival from what was once one of the richest-endowed countries on earth.

Until 1984, the bankers lent more to the poor countries than they got back in interest. By 1988, the 'return' (a basic concept of the free market) was turning the flow in the other direction. That year the poor countries paid back $50 billion more than they borrowed.

The poor of the world are not found only in the non-developing countries, the poorer countries. There are large numbers of them in the richer countries too. They too are increasing as the market system—the one which claims it matches production to people—gets more successful. By 1988, in the United States of America, the land of the free market, there were 32 million people (including one-fifth of all American children) living below what the government itself said was the poverty line. In the great free market boom of 1980 to 1984, the real incomes of the poorest 40 per cent of the population fell by 3 per cent.

Between 1981 and 1987, the US federal government showed its commitment to the free market by cutting its spending on housing from eight billion dollars to three billion. Housing for the poor, which had to be subsidised, was cut from 20,000 units a year in the 1970s to 5000 a year in the 1980s.

Prime minister Margaret Thatcher pursued exactly the same free-market policies in Britain, with exactly the same results. Perhaps the most astonishing feature of the great decade of the free market in Britain was the increase in the numbers of poor and homeless people. At the start of the decade, 6.1 million people were living on or below the level at which they were entitled to supplementary benefit. By 1985, this had grown to 9.4 million, and has been growing ever since.

As in the United States, Margaret Thatcher's interpretation of the free market is that only people who can *afford* expensive housing really want or need houses. Under her guidance, councils have been almost completely prevented from building subsidised houses to rent. For the first time since the 1880s the streets of central London are filled with hungry, homeless people, begging for money for a meal and preferring to risk the elements rather than spend their pittance on an insanitary and dangerous dosshouse.

This astonishing increase in the starving millions, with all the indescribable wretchedness and hopelessness which goes with it, is the chief achievement of the free market in its Great Decade. Its supporters, led by the American president and the British prime minister, have from time to time harked back to that famous dictum of Christ: 'the poor ye have always with you'. Jesus Christ, who, if he existed, was certainly poor, seemed to be saying that since there was not enough to go round, some people were bound to end up with next to nothing. Like so many of the remarks attributed to him, this one has been taken up by supporters of the free market everywhere to blame poverty on the poor themselves: on their own fecklessness and inability to 'better themselves'.

All this disguises the central difference between the poor at the time that Jesus Christ was said to be living, and the poor today. It was true two thousand years ago that there wasn't enough to go round, so some people were bound to be poor. In 1990, however, there is enough to go round; more than enough to go round. To adapt another of Christ's phrases, it is the triumph of the market system that although the world is full of plenty, the market ensures that it is distributed among them that hath, and withheld from them that hath not.

A billion and a quarter people cannot get enough to eat. Yet there is, easily, the capacity to produce enough food to feed the world's population twice over. There is enough food actually produced today to feed everyone on earth. Edgar Owens, of the United States Agency for International Development, told a conference in November 1974:

> If the arable land of our planet was cultivated as efficiently as farms in Holland, the planet would feed 67 billion people, seventeen times as many people as are now alive.

That might be rather excessive, so, to give a better and more practical picture, here is the Food and Agriculture Organisation (FAO) of the United Nations, in 1976:

> There would be no difficulty whatever with the existing knowledge and resources in doubling food production.

Another United Nations organisation calculated that 0.5 per cent of world spending on weapons of destruction, often mass destruction, would be enough to provide the investment in agriculture in the stricken continent of Africa sufficient to produce enough food easily to feed the entire African population. 0.5 per cent! A tiny fragment of the money devoted to killing could save the lives of millions and millions of people! Yet the 'free market' keeps it firmly locked up in bombs and bullets. At the same time it has ruthlessly cut production in the fertile farmlands of the United States of America. It has even launched a campaign to cut off funds from the United Nations agencies which have the effrontery to reveal the full horror of free-market priorities.

Everywhere, the discrepancy gapes so wide that even the blindest believer in the free market cannot avoid it. The human race now has at its disposal more than enough technology, raw materials, knowledge and imagination to fulfil everyone's basic needs without difficulty. As the man from the FAO said, there would be 'no problem' in doubling food production, no problem for that matter in providing the people of the world with food, clothing, shelter, heat and light, not to mention education, health, and transport.

The figures for potential production are there in all the statistics. All human beings could be progressing in comfort and plenty, cooperating internationally to safeguard future generations from war, and diverting the war-making machines which have been handed down to us by the free market into building a safe and comfortable world. There is no need whatever for the poor to be with us now, let alone always. A flick on the tiller of the industries and farms of the world could wipe out poverty forever.

None of this is idealistic illusion. It is simple common sense, based on the statistics of what is now produced.

How is it, then, that our free marketeers insist on policies which condemn such enormous numbers of human beings to ruin?

The answer has its roots in the other major social development of the 1980s: the enrichment of the rich. This has been so stupendous as to defy statistics. In all the countries of the world, including the poor countries, the rich have been enjoying the greatest bonanza ever. The top 10 per cent of incomes in the United States of America, already far, far ahead of the rest of the population, increased their share of the wealth by another 7 per cent. In Britain the value of shares on the stock exchange multiplied five times between 1983 and 1987, and even the stock exchange crash of 1987 did not stop the fantastic accumulation of riches for the already super-rich.

Old-fashioned ideas, especially in publicly owned state industries, that the chairmen and managing directors should keep their earnings down as an example to their workers, vanished. As the public utilities in Britain were turned, 'in the interests of competition', from public monopolies to private monopolies, the chairmen and directors rewarded themselves for what they assessed as their 'true worth'—and promptly doubled and tripled their salaries. Enormous fortunes were flaunted by the millionaires' press. At the start of the decade there were only a handful of billionaires in the world: at the end there were 157. Millionaires increased four times—from half a million to two million.

Tax-cutting everywhere aided the process. The highest rate of income tax in Britain was cut from 83 per cent at the start of the decade to 40 per cent at the end. With this went cuts in all the taxes which affected the rich: corporation tax, capital gains tax, inheritance tax. The poll tax, in abolishing property rates, put further millions into the pockets of the already rich.

David Stockman, who had been brought in by US president Reagan to organise the tax-cutting spree, became himself disgusted. 'Do you realise the greed that came to the forefront?' he wrote to a friend. 'The hogs were really feeding. The greed level, the level of opportunism, just got out of control.' A film called **Wall Street**, whose purpose was to demonstrate how vile and vulgar were the rich when compared with working people, was greeted with wide acclaim, and even applause. The slogan of the hero in the film, based on a standard Wall Street marauder, was 'Greed is Good'. It was adopted by governments, stock exchanges and bourses, and wherever else people gathered to make money out of someone else's effort.

The enrichment of the rich led to comparisons which were noticed even by the most liberal institutes. The Worldwatch Institute report on the decade set out to make 'practical proposals' for helping the poor:

> Americans spend five billion dollars each year on special diets to lower their calorie consumption, while 400 million people around the world are so undernourished that their bodies and minds are deteriorating. As water from a single spring in France is bottled and shipped to the prosperous around the globe, nearly two billion people drink and bathe in water contaminated with deadly parasites and pathogens.

Since the rich own almost all the newspapers and control almost all the television stations, these ugly comparisons are seldom made.

On the rare occasions when the rich are called to account, they accuse their accusers of jealousy. They claim two major justifications for their wealth. The first is that ability and enterprise has to be rewarded. The rich, they say, are rich because of their contribution to society, which is exceptional and therefore deserves to be rewarded exceptionally.

Most rich people, however, are rich through no ability of their own. A recent survey of wealth in Britain found that the greatest amount of wealth is still owned by people who have inherited it. In other words, they are rich because their fathers, grandfathers or ancestors, with a great spurt of initiative and enterprise, died; leaving all their wealth—which was almost certainly acquired by some form of privilege or plunder—to their children, grandchildren and so on for evermore.

A lot of very rich people have no recognisable ability—with inherited wealth you don't need ability. Many are rich precisely because they have no sensitivity or intellectual depth: they can read a financial balance sheet while ignoring the human exploitation that the profit figures represent. Such a man, for instance, was Roy Thomson, who became boss of one of the world's greatest paper and publishing chains. Howard Hughes was another from the same mould. He started life as a playboy and ended it as a lunatic. He designed a plane which crashed and made a film which no one went to see. Because of an ability to be at the right place at the right time, and to read a balance sheet, he became head of a vast financial and industrial empire, and was able to nominate the president of the United States.

The new millionaires who emerged in the 1980s, almost to a man, are people without any noticeable skill, intellect or ability. They are expert only at playing the stock market or sacking workers —the two activities most likely to make a fast million.

The second justification for vast riches has been used by the high and mighty throughout history. It is that the wealth of rich men rubs off on poor people too. This argument is also taken from the bible, which tells the story of a beggar who sat at the foot of the rich man's table so that he could catch the crumbs which fell from it. The sophisticated argument of the rich man was that if there were no rich man, there would be no crumbs.

Slightly embarrassed by the 'crumbs' metaphor, the rich today have invented a new, just as disgusting, notion to justify their riches. They call it the 'trickle down' theory. The richer the rich, it is argued, the more will 'trickle down' to the poor. No one can explain exactly how this trickling down works—and the facts of the past ten years prove the opposite. While the rich have gorged themselves, as we have seen, the poor have got poorer.

Indeed, the pattern throughout the whole of this century is exactly the opposite of what the rich pretend. The richer the rich have got, the poorer the poor have become. When the rich get their own way, as they did in the 1980s, the poor get less—not just in money but in all the other things which hold out some hope: free health, free schools, free recreation facilities, social security payments—and so on.

This pattern brings us to two simple truths about the world we live in: exploitation and class. The rich are rich not because of their ability, or because they allow so much to 'trickle down', or for any other reason save that they have robbed other people's labour.

There would be no wealth at all if no one worked. Labour is essential to everything that is produced. The rich have got rich because they have swiped a proportion of the value of the workers' labour, and because they use that surplus for one purpose only: to increase their own wealth, power and privilege.

This exploitation of labour, by a class of people who have grown rich because of it, is as central a characteristic of society today as it ever was. The 'market' is the economic mechanism by which this system works. It claims to be able to identify what is wanted or needed, and then to produce it. It claims an 'economic discipline' which only produces where a profit can be made. If something makes a profit, it is selling and therefore it is needed. If it doesn't make a profit, it isn't needed or wanted and therefore shouldn't be made.

You may of course need something very badly, but not have the money to buy it—in which case you don't count in the market. Millions of starving people are in this predicament.

The market is driven not by reason or need, but by irrationality and greed. In each new burst of investment workers are taken on, and there is a short boom. When the investment is over, workers are laid off and more goods come on the market at prices they can't afford. So there is a slump.

This switchback ride from boom to slump has been going on ever since the beginning of capitalism. For thirty years after the Second World War, capitalists started slapping each other on the backs and telling themselves they had overcome the tendency of their system to crisis. But since the mid-1970s the crises have returned with a vengeance.

Marx described the market system as a mixture of despotism and anarchy. The anarchy can be seen all over the world today. Vast investment programmes during booms are suddenly scrapped in slump, and whole communities are wrecked in the process. In the early 1970s the British steel industry invested for an annual production target of 30 million tons of steel. Whole new plants and factories were built for the purpose—only to be scrapped when the production targets were 'scaled down' (thanks to the market system) to 16 million and then 10 million tons.

In 1972 a vast new investment programme was started to set the British coal industry 'on its feet again'. New washeries were built and pits renovated. Then came the 1980s, and the prospect of cheaper coal from places where the workers were more poorly paid—South Africa, for instance, or Poland—and the same industry closed nearly 100 pits and sacked two-thirds of the miners.

No one knows what will happen next, who will suffer next. Capitalism is blind to the future. Its forecasters and experts had no idea, for instance, that a stock exchange crash was coming in October 1987. **Fortune** magazine had commissioned a special feature on 'The End of Socialism', which had to be tactfully postponed when the crash took everyone by surprise. Milton Friedman, the arch-apostle of the market, confessed after the crash:

> Nobody knows what causes these panics. The causes are psychological and no one understands them. I don't know what caused the Great Tulip Bubble, nor last week's panic.

Since the central drive of the market is to enrich the rich at others' expense, its madness and megalomania rivals that of any gang of rulers in all history. President Houphouet-Boigny of the Ivory Coast, one of the poorest countries on earth, recently built an air-conditioned Catholic cathedral which is bigger even than St Peter's in Rome. The stained glass (nine acres of it) came from France and the marble was the most expensive in the world—from Italy. The cathedral cost 200 million dollars, more than any major investment ever made in that desperately poor country—where, incidentally, only a tenth of the population is Roman Catholic. 'The market' operates in the Ivory Coast—yet who can say that the Catholic cathedral there is any less monstrous than Ceausescu's palace in Romania, where state capitalism was the ruling system?

At any rate, one madness leads to another. In 1980, another desperately poor African country, Sierra Leone, forked out two-thirds of its entire annual budget on pomp and circumstance for the Organisation of African Unity summit meeting.

The despotism is even more obvious than the anarchy. The wealthiest companies in the market are every day merging themselves into vaster and vaster multinational corporations. Most of these multinationals have more wealth and power than most of the countries in the world. They are organised hierarchically—from the top downwards. Everyone looks for inspiration to the top. The structure of a multinational company in the market system is every bit as much a 'command structure' as were the old governments of Eastern Europe. The Tariff Commission as early as 1973 saw what was happening:

> In the largest and most sophisticated multinational corporations, planning and subsequent monitoring of plan fulfilment have reached a scope and level of detail that, ironically, resembles more than superficially the national planning procedures of Communist countries.

Ironically indeed. The so-called Communist governments operated by command, promotion and fear. So do the multinationals. They have not the slightest interest or concern about anything except the profitability and success of their company. They proceed in the name of the market to exploit the world's natural resources without thought for the future, to root up the rain forests and poison the world's atmosphere. They have not the slightest concern for the social implications of what they do. They constantly cut safety corners, endangering their customers and the public at large.

The Boeing aircraft disaster on the M1 motorway in 1988, the fire at Kings Cross tube station in London, the capsize of the ferry so appropriately called *The Herald of Free Enterprise*—all these and many other disasters were the direct result of the capitalists' putting profit first and their consequent perennial contempt for the vast mass of human beings.

The period of economic crisis which began 20 years ago is by far the worst which capitalism has encountered since the Great Depression and mass poverty of the 1930s. In the 1980s, there was a burst of capitalist confidence and an effective surrender by many of its opponents. As the decade drew to a close, however, and as the real truth about the market system was brought home to employed workers (as well as to the unemployed and homeless who felt it first and keenest), the revolt against it began to spread.

In 1990, Margaret Thatcher's British miracle looks pitiful. She had one policy and one policy alone to deal with the economic crisis: old-fashioned recession, and mass unemployment. She used this to the full when she first came to office in 1979. Many predicted she would never get away with it, but she had strong support from the true supporters of the market system. Sir Keith Joseph, her economic *guru*, told his chauffeur: 'We're hoping for three million unemployed, perhaps four.' They got their unemployed, and so by the oldest device known to capitalism 'squeezed inflation out of the system'. The recession passed, a small investment boom started, and once again wages and prices began to rise.

Confronted with rising inflation once again, Margaret Thatcher and her colleagues reach once more for the same old button. Each month they look longingly at the figures, praying for higher unemployment, another recession and a chance to squeeze inflation out of the system in time to recover before the next general election.

Even if she does not win that election, Margaret Thatcher's government has served her class well. She has given them telephones, electricity, gas and water to make profits out of. She has ended the slender democracy whereby Labour-controlled local councils could raise rates on property and provide services for the poor. She boasts of 'enormously increased productivity', which means of course that the workers have worked harder to produce more wealth, and the beneficiaries—as always—have been their employers.

The triumph of market capitalism in Britain was celebrated at the employers' CBI conference in 1990, when speaker after speaker went to the rostrum to plead for lower wages. Rises of 9 per cent (with inflation running at 9.4 per cent) were, they declared unanimously, intolerable. On the last day of the conference the average pay rise for British directors was announced. It was 33 per cent.

At the end of the decade, the market system represented by Thatcher, Reagan and their multinationals finally made it into the heartland of the former Communist bloc in Eastern Europe: Poland. The legal correspondent of the **Financial Times** went there to see what had happened. He reported, suitably enough, on 1 May:

> For the first-time visitor to Warsaw it comes as a bit of a shock—not the large number of spanking new Mercedes cars (though it takes a little while to adjust to that), not Stalin's Palace of Culture, which rises above the city's commercial centre like an overblown wedding cake, but the shops. They are full of goods. What has happened to the

long queues and empty shelves about which we have read so much? They have gone, it seems—the inevitable consequence of the Polish government's drive towards a free market economy.

The lifting of price controls and cuts in state subsidies to industry have cut the purchasing power of Polish wages by a third since January. Prices have risen so fast that the average Pole can no longer afford to buy.

For the Polish workers the long dark night of a state-capitalist system, where there was nothing in the shops for money to buy, had ended in the long dark dawn of free enterprise, where there was plenty in the shops, but no money to buy it. They and all the other working people of the world must be wondering if there is an alternative.

5: THE NEW EMINENCE

'In bourgeois society, living labour is but a means to increase accumulated labour. In communist society, accumulated labour is but a means to widen, to enrich, to promote the existence of the labourer.'

—*Karl Marx and Frederick Engels,* **The Communist Manifesto.**

THE ALTERNATIVE is socialism. The word has been so misused for so long that it is worth re-stating its basic principles.

Socialism means that the means of production are owned and controlled by society so that what is produced can be shared out according to people's needs. Socialism is founded on the idea of equality, which means that most people will get the same.

The basic objections to such a system have been the same ever since it was first conceived, and the arguments against them are still very much the same too.

'Human nature', it is said, is fundamentally opposed to such a system, since human nature is selfish and greedy. In the end the 'old Adam' will out, and will wreck any egalitarian system.

Poor 'old Adam' is always hauled out to justify the horrors of capitalism. Two hundred years of exploitation don't sound so bad if you can put it down to human nature. In fact, however, people's natures are not at all like those of speculators in the City of London. Indeed it is hard, even in the City of London, to come across people whose natures are dominated entirely by greed, selfishness and a hatred of the rest of the human race. There are at least as many examples in everyday life of generosity and self-sacrifice as there are of selfishness and greed.

How people behave depends very much on the kind of society they live in. If the society beckons forward the greedy and the selfish, if it offers them great riches and privileges in return for collaboration in exploiting others, if it criminalises solidarity (as the Tory trade union laws have done), then people will lose their confidence in one another, shrink into their shells and denounce their neighbours. If, on the other hand, society welcomes those who act and think as part of the community, people's confidence in themselves and in one another will grow and the dark side of their natures will diminish.

The notion of equality is greeted by Tories with shouts of 'you'll make us all the same'. They insist that socialists do not recognise the variety in human beings and will reduce all individual character to an indistinguishable mass. All art, architecture, literature, media and so on will, they tell us, be the same.

This sameness and uniformity, however, are increasingly the characteristics of monopoly capitalism. All around us privately controlled mass media and mass production churn out things that assume that their consumers are all the same. Differences and distinctions between human beings are far more likely to blossom in a society which rewards everybody equally and does not single out a few for special treatment. As **The Communist Manifesto** puts it: 'In place of the old society... we will have an association in which the free development of each will be the condition for the free development of all.'

Another argument against the idea of equality is that it will discourage skills. This argument usually starts with a question: 'Would you pay a brain surgeon the same as a dustman?' If you reply 'Yes', the argument is pressed home. 'Aha! This will produce a society where there are millions of dustmen and no brain surgeons.' The brain surgeon, it is assumed, will not study or practise for his or her skills unless the rewards for this are ten or twenty or preferably fifty times that of a dustman. People would just as soon hump a dustbin on their backs as be a brain surgeon for equal money.

The socialist argument is that people are far more likely to do what they want to do, and what they are best able to do, if the reward for everything is roughly the same than if a fortunate minority are beckoned to a specific set of skills by huge rewards.

One of the propaganda triumphs of capitalism in the 20th century has been its association of socialism with austerity. Somehow capitalism, a system which has produced all through its history mass poverty on the most disgusting scale, manages to condemn its alternative as a society in which no one will have very much. The socialists, it is said, are after your possessions, your video, your TV, your sticks of furniture, probably even your daughters. Lock them all up! The Reds are coming!

The socialists reply that we are on the verge of a world of plenty. All around us are the signs that we can produce more than enough for everyone. If production is planned and its products shared fairly, there is no reason why anyone should be short of anything—nor why the environment should be polluted and destroyed in the process. The priority is to cut out the dirty work and the drudgery, to devote far more of people's lives to education, recreation and leisure.

As for possessions, the whole point of the public ownership of the means of production is that more is produced and shared out, not less. The British socialist John Strachey (when he was still a Marxist) put this very well:

> The point is that there are two different sorts of private property. The one is private property in the means of production: private property in a factory or a mine, or in the land. And the other sort is private property in consumers' goods, in food and clothing and furniture, in houses, in motor cars, in gardens, in labour-saving devices, in access to amusements, in every sort of thing which we actually use and consume... It ought to be impossible to mix them up. For there is one rule for distinguishing between them. Private property of the first sort carries an income with it... Private property of the second sort does not carry an income with it. The economic system which is currently called socialism involves abolishing the first sort of private property in order to increase vastly the second sort of property.

These arguments for socialism and against capitalism have gone on all through the century, and are just as strong today as they ever were.

A planned economy, so that production is for need, not profit, and equality, so that the goods produced are distributed fairly, are essential for socialism. But if the argument stops there, as it so often does, the project has a fatal weakness—which the history of our century has exposed. A centralised plan, and something which calls itself equality, can be imposed from above, without the active participation of the working people. They have been so imposed in Russia and Eastern Europe. Similarly, Labour parties, especially in Britain, have tried to impose these things in the industrial countries of the West.

Both experiments have called themselves socialist (though neither Communist nor Labour parties are inclined to use the word any more). Both have made a mockery of the planned economy and a sick joke of equality. The reason is simple. In both cases 'socialism' was attained or attempted without the involvement of the exploited class. The soul of socialism, the self-emancipation of the working class and the democratic control of society from below, was missing. What masqueraded as socialism was either state capitalism, or 'reforms' which left capitalism intact, if not stronger.

To go back to where we started, Karl Marx was (perhaps excessively) reluctant to provide detailed accounts of what socialism would be like. Marxist scholars have picked through his writing to try to find The Complete Definition of Socialism. There isn't one. There isn't more than the odd sentence holding out a principle or an idea. Marx was certain that socialism would not come according to a prescription laid down by him or anyone else. Socialism could only come when the exploited class rose against its rulers. The industries had to be seized by the workers. The state which ran society for the rich had to be broken up and replaced with something completely different.

If socialism were only a planned economy and equality, then well-meaning socialists would think they could command it or legislate for it—it wouldn't matter much which. When Beatrice and Sidney Webb, two grand old British parliamentarians, went to Russia in 1935 and beheld the full horror of Stalinist Russia in mass production, they loved it. They wrote a stunningly tedious book entitled **Soviet Communism: A new civilisation?** After thinking about the title, they removed the question mark. Here was a planned economy and something which looked like equality, imposed from above. Beatrice and Sidney (who was by that time called Lord Passfield) reckoned they could bring that sort of society about in Britain with laws that would pass through both houses of parliament.

The importance of the essential ingredient of socialism, which both Stalin and the Webbs left out, cannot be overstated. It is its democratic spirit, its control from below, its conversion of the cooperation which takes place in production into control of that production. There is about this process not a breath of tyranny. Freedom and democracy are vital to it. Fred Engels put it like this:

> In making itself the master of all the means of production, in order to use them in accordance with a social plan, society puts an end to the former subjection of men to their own means of production. It goes without saying that society cannot itself be free unless each individual is free. The old mode of production must therefore be revolutionised from top to bottom. Its place must be taken by an organisation of production in which, on the one hand, no individual can put on to other persons his share of the productive labour... and in which on the other hand productive labour, instead of being a means to the subjection of men, will become a means to their emancipation, by giving each individual the opportunity to develop and exercise all his faculties.

There it is in a nutshell: the planned economy, the equality and the revolutionary emancipation all rolled into one. Without the third element, the other two become not an incomplete socialism but the opposite of it.

The subjection of human beings by the organisation of productive labour has increased a hundredfold since Engels wrote that passage. The greater the exploitation, the more miserable the lot of so many workers, and the greater the case for socialism. The worst crime of capitalism is its enslavement and corruption of the human spirit. It binds that spirit to the yoke of productive labour, lobs it back and forth between boom and slump, insults and degrades it as if it were no more than part of the machinery. 'We are,' says the Guatamalan peasant in the film **El Norte**, 'just arms and legs for them.'

What a waste it all is! How many men, women and children are flushed down the pan of history without even for a day savouring their own abilities, dreams and joys! Sitting in a churchyard long ago, contemplating the gravestones and writing a rather boring poem which has been learned by rote by infuriated school students ever since, Thomas Gray was suddenly struck by outrage at all the wasted talent buried there:

> Chill Penury repress'd their noble rage,
> And froze the genial current of the soul.
> Full many a gem of purest ray serene
> The dark unfathom'd caves of ocean bear:
> Full many a flower is born to blush unseen
> And waste its sweetness on the desert air.

Many, many years later Leon Trotsky, when he'd got a taste of what is possible after a revolution, wrote even more poetically of what can be achieved once people are in control of property, and not the other way round:

> Lastly, in the deepest and dimmest recesses of the unconscious, there lurks the nature of man himself. On it, clearly, he will concentrate the supreme effort of his mind and of his creative initiative. Mankind will not have ceased to crawl before God, Tsar and Capital only in order to surrender meekly to dark laws of heredity and blind sexual selection. Man will strive to control his own feelings, to raise his instincts to the height of his conscious mind, and to bring clarity into them; to channel his will-power into his unconscious depths; and in this way he will lift himself into new eminence.

6: A WORLD TO WIN

The spirit that lifts the slave before his Lord
Stalks through the capitals of armed kings,
And spreads its ensign in the wilderness.
—*Shelley*.

BACK WE COME with a bump to where we started: Margaret Thatcher's Britain in the early 1990s. Her game is up. The mixture of fear and hypnosis which seems to have struck people down isn't working any more. Most people want her out. They are sick of right-wing government, and they want a change.

What sort of change? Rather like the masses in Eastern Europe at the end of 1989, most people seem happy with a minor change. They want the government out, but they do not want too sharp a shift in the other direction. The New Model Labour Party under Neil Kinnock has become the focus of hope for most people who want political change. A Kinnock-led Labour government, it is argued, would improve things—marginally. It would scrap the poll tax, increase child benefits and old-age pensions. It would build a few more council houses. It would spend a little more on public transport. It would usher in a slightly fairer and more decent society without changing anything too fast.

How far they have come, these Labourites, from the hopes of their origins! How mean and miserable are their aspirations compared even with what their most right-wing supporters were saying thirty or forty years ago!

In the 1950s and 1960s, political pundits started to talk about 'consensus politics'. They detected a basic agreement between most politicians, whatever their party, about what could be achieved by parliamentary politics. The consensus at that time was called 'Butskellism', after the leading Tory R A Butler and the leader of the Labour Party Hugh Gaitskell. Their 'consensus' agreed on the need for a National Health Service, a declining private sector in education, a certain amount of nationalisation, full employment, strong and free trade unions. On the Labour side, the new consensus was expressed by Anthony Crosland in **The Future of Socialism**, published in 1956. He prophesied permanent industrial peace:

> One cannot imagine a deliberate offensive alliance between government and employers... with all the brutal paraphernalia of wage cuts, national lock-outs and anti-union legislation.

He could not imagine it, but it happened very soon. Crosland's unimaginable horror became the reality of the 1980s.

Crosland was even more optimistic about the economic future:

> I no longer regard questions of growth and efficiency as being, on a long view, of primary importance to socialism. We stand in Britain on the threshold of mass abundance.

For Crosland, the old slumps and booms of pre-war capitalism, with all their dreadful consequences—mass unemployment, poverty, welfare cuts and so on—were gone forever. Somehow, without even knowing how they did it, modern politicians had rid themselves of the old problems and could turn their attention to new ones. Crosland's socialist future concentrated on different matters. 'We need,' he wrote,

> not only higher exports and old-age pensions, but more open-air cafés, brighter and gayer streets at night, later closing hours for public houses, more local repertory theatres, better and more hospitable hoteliers and restaurateurs, brighter and cleaner eating houses, more riverside cafés, more pleasure gardens on the Battersea model, more murals and pictures in public places, better designs for furniture and pottery and women's clothes, statues in the centre of new housing estates, better-designed new street lamps and telephone kiosks and so on *ad infinitum*.

On the whole, Tories agreed with this. They liked the idea of a fully employed capitalist Britain where employers and workers, Tories and Labour Party people could mingle contentedly in better-designed riverside cafés.

The consensus started to break up in the mid-1970s. In 1975 Tory MPs elected a new leader, the strident right-winger Margaret Thatcher. She openly attacked the consensus, calling for a return to the naked capitalism of the Victorian era. Nationalisation, public spending of all kinds, council houses, state schools and National Health Service hospitals were all at risk from the new ideology of the right. This extraordinary choice had nothing to do with personalities. By any definition, Thatcher's chief rival, William Whitelaw, had a more congenial personality. Thatcher's election was one of the signs that Crosland's prophecy was wrong. Capitalism had not solved its problems. The old cycle of slumps and booms was re-emerging. Unemployment had topped a million, and was still rising. The class war, written off so often, was back on the agenda.

The Labour government of the time did little to resist this new trend. Indeed their chancellor of the exchequer, Denis Healey, put into practice the very monetarism and the very cuts in public spending which Crosland had said were unimaginable. These were the policies which ensured that there would be no new council housing estates to put Tony Crosland's statues in, no cheap eating houses to make brighter and cleaner and fewer telephone kiosks on which to improve the design.

The process has continued through the 1980s and into the 1990s. Thatcher, this time in office, has led the way and the Labour Party has followed. Today we have a new consensus, based on unemployment rather than full employment, on free market capitalism rather than a mixed economy, and on an acceptance of the right to be rich rather than a right not to be poor.

This huge slippage in aims, aspirations and policies is a warning of what is to come. At no time since the war has Labour called the tune in politics. Throughout, it has responded to events, shamefacedly shuffled off what it now calls the 'baggage' of its heritage, and settled for a new society which, in all but the faces on the government front bench, is largely indistinguishable from the old one.

The sheer opportunism involved in this process has astonished even those who have pushed it on. The most hideous example is Labour's attitude to British nuclear weapons. At two general elections—1983 and 1987—Labour argued that the British government should stop making and stockpiling these weapons. They were, Labour argued, useless, expensive and an encouragement to all other belligerent nations who wanted their own bombs. It was a clear policy, easily argued, at one time shared by a majority of the people, again and again passed at party conferences and enthusiastically endorsed by the enormous majority of Labour Party members.

A mighty campaign against this anti-nuclear policy was set in train by the Tories. Labour, they said, was leaving Britain 'defenceless' against the only enemy country which had nuclear weapons: Russia. The campaign, so the polls pronounced, damaged Labour in the elections. Accordingly, after 1987, the Labour leaders set their minds to changing it.

Their problem, however, was that Russia, the former 'enemy', was now rapidly becoming a 'friend'. There were now no 'enemy' nations with nuclear weapons! The last half-argument for keeping them was gone. Yet doggedly the Labour leaders constructed a 'defence policy' which was based on keeping nuclear weapons for possible use against... er... no one in particular.

The new policy was warmly endorsed by the Labour Party conference. The best explanation came from a delegate called Sylvia Heal, who said she was quite prepared to sacrifice her former allegiance to CND and her continued belief in the case for scrapping nuclear weapons in exchange for winning the next election. What mattered, she said, was parliamentary power. She was able to realise this earlier than she expected when she won the Mid-Staffordshire by-election in 1990—the best by-election result for Labour in all its history.

Sylvia Heal's speech is echoed everywhere on the left and half-left today. People declare themselves sick of 'grand ideas which never get us anywhere'. They openly applaud the trimming and erasing of their own long-standing beliefs and commitments. So great is the hysteria about winning the next election, so totally does it carry everything before it, that every word, every policy, almost every thought of Labour MPs and their supporters is measured by only one yardstick: will it lose votes? Thus Labour policy is devised not by rational men and women with their own distinctive ideas, but by the opinion pollsters.

The decline in Labour's aspirations and the weakness of its policies become, by this token, positive advantages. People say (without even realising how cynical they sound) that 'if Labour promises a little, it won't sell out.' They stress again and again that they will be satisfied with 'just a little'. They denounce their few socialist critics as saboteurs of practical and possible reform.

At the root of all these arguments is the notion that the political spring which waters society is parliament; that political measures, reformist or reactionary, all flow from parliament and therefore nothing can be done to emancipate labour unless parliament is won for Labour. If Labour is elected, laws and measures flow from parliament which are friendly to labour. If Labour loses, those laws and measures will be hostile to labour. It follows that everything must be subordinated to securing a Labour government.

The briefest glance at post-war British history proves the entire argument false. There was full employment during the Tory years of 1955-1964; and heavy unemployment in the Labour years 1975-1978. In the 1950s and early 1960s the Tories built hundreds of thousands of council houses, and maintained a completely free National Health Service (not to mention completely free school meals). The school leaving age was raised when the secretary of state for education was Margaret Thatcher. Far more public spending was committed to railways and coal mines by Edward Heath's Tory government in 1972 than in any year of the ensuing Labour government. And it was not a Tory government, but a Labour one, which was the first since the war to propose laws to curb the trade unions.

The pattern of reform and reaction does not follow the pattern of elections and the change of governments. There are other forces at work far stronger than the elected governments. Every Labour government in history has come to office pledged to end unemployment, or at least reduce it. Every Labour government in history has left office with unemployment higher than when it was elected.

The rise and fall of the 'business cycle', capitalism's 'booms and slumps', do not wait to see which government is in office. They follow economic laws over which parliamentary laws have nothing but the remotest control. Governments can shell out money for the unemployed, but only enough to keep them worse off than the very lowest-paid of the employed. They can employ a few, train a few. But no government can alter the rules of a catastrophic economic system.

When Mrs Thatcher said 'You cannot buck the market', she was explaining not only Labour's impotence but her own. When in May 1990 the newly privatised British Steel said it would close down the strip mill at Ravenscraig in Scotland, Mrs Thatcher's own government, in the shape of the wimpish secretary of state for Scotland Malcolm Rifkind, tried to dissuade them. (There are few enough Tory votes in Scotland already). The chairman of British Steel, who had been raised to his new prominence by the Tories' privatisation policies, sent his former benefactor packing. 'We are not,' he told Rifkind haughtily, 'responsible to the government —but to our shareholders.' Not even Thatcher or Rifkind could save 10,000 jobs in Scotland when the market dictated otherwise.

The market and the struggle between classes which it creates lay down the priorities for society. If there is full employment, and the trade unions are strong, they fight for decent housing and welfare. This is just as likely to happen under a Tory government as under Labour. Houses, hospitals and schools then get built for the masses, because the employers and the moneylenders can afford them. But when capitalism is in crisis, the battle for every penny intensifies. Unemployment weakens the unions, and it is the employers who feel strong, militant and confident.

Of course, employers prefer a Tory government and workers prefer a Labour government. Of course, it is more difficult for either side to proceed if there is a hostile government in office. But equally, a strong working class can make gains from a Tory government and a confident ruling class will play havoc with a Labour government.

There is absolutely nothing inevitable about reforms under a Labour government. From the moment the votes are counted and a Labour government is declared in office, a huge war is launched on that government by the class with economic power. The war takes many different forms: investment strikes by the holders of capital, a run on sterling organised by the treasurers of multinational companies, violent campaigns in the media, rebellions by the military, the police and the judiciary. There have been plenty of examples of all of these since 1945: the runs on sterling in 1966 and 1975 changed the whole course of the Labour governments then recently elected; the judges staged a revolt over comprehensive schools and over trade union blacking in 1976; the media campaigned viciously against Harold Wilson in 1967; the military in Northern Ireland refused orders from a Labour government in 1974.

These are just examples. There is no limit to their scope. The smallest morsel of reform will be snatched from Labour if its class enemies believe they can get away with it.

In January 1968, as the Labour government under Harold Wilson negotiated with the International Monetary Fund over public spending cuts after devaluation of the pound, a deal seemed almost struck. It involved hundreds of millions of pounds of cuts in crucial areas of public spending.

Then the IMF, in the shape of brilliant young men from investment banks in Massachusetts, made their final demand. They wanted prescription charges imposed on medicines. Wilson's ministers begged, wheedled, and offered all sorts of other cuts in exchange. Free medicine, they whined, was the sacred cow of the Labour Party. Of all the policies they had introduced when they first came into office four years previously, they were proudest of their removal of the health charges. The great Aneurin Bevan, along with Harold Wilson, had resigned from a former government on the issue. Could they please, they implored, be spared the health charges?

The IMF, sensing its certain victory, and knowing well how important it was to humiliate the government in the eyes of its socialist supporters, stuck firm. Though the health charges were only peanuts in the context of total government spending—some £8 million—it insisted on them. The Labour ministers surrendered. A great portrait of them with their hands in the air should be unveiled at Labour Party headquarters and dedicated to all those who suppress their socialist opinions so that the next Labour government can do the 'little things'.

If reforms are determined not by the rhythm of elections or the colour of the government but by the rise and fall of class confidence, it follows that the weaker Labour's policies are the more likely it is that they will be abandoned. R H Tawney, a social-democratic thinker and writer with more socialism in his little finger than there is in Kinnock's whole shadow cabinet, once warned his Labour colleagues that they could not skin a tiger claw by claw. He might have gone on to say that you cannot, by putting your head into the tiger's mouth, turn him into a vegetarian.

Tawney's tiger metaphor illustrates the central argument against the fashionable emphasis on the next general election.

It is not just that the reforms may be illusory, nor even that hundreds of thousands of socialists will be disillusioned and depressed when the reforms they hoped for are not achieved, but that the fixation on reforms through parliament disarms the real movement for change.

Parliamentary politics are necessarily passive. In order to achieve that vital parliamentary majority, politicians must forever preach passivity. Any protest movement which mobilises people against their rulers disturbs the peaceful pace of the parliamentary reformers. However much in theory they support a cause, they feel bound to confine it to a constitutional cage. Strikes, the most effective weapons in the hands of the dispossessed, are anathema to the parliamentary socialist. The same goes for demonstrations, agitations, even propaganda and thought. The central principle of parliamentary activity is that change is most effectively brought by politicians *from above*. Whether those politicians are in office or out of it, therefore, it is best for them if people who are not politicians keep quiet and lie down.

Thus in the great miners' strike of 1984-5, the theme from the Labour leaders was that the miners should cool it. The mass solidarity action necessary to win the strike was discouraged. Miners were pressed to stay at home and not to go to the picket line.

By the same token, the great agitation against the poll tax in early 1990 was constantly cut down and insulted by leading Labour politicians. The enormous demonstration of 31 March, which was attacked by the police and which refused to dissolve under the attack, was assailed on all sides in parliament, most of all by Labour. In the council chambers, local Labour politicians developed an acute form of political schizophrenia. On the one hand they explained that they were against the poll tax, that the poll tax was unfair, monstrous, the worst attack on the poor since the days of Wat Tyler.

On the other, they called on their supporters to pay the tax, and threatened them with bailiffs, fines and even prison if they refused to do so. Gradually, the schizophrenia wore off. The councillors became first and foremost, unconditionally and militantly, collectors of the tax rather than opponents of it. A chasm opened up between those who wanted to fight the tax by not paying it, and the leaders of the party who opposed the tax but suppressed their opposition in their determination not to rock the Labour Party boat on its voyage to the next general election.

As Rosa Luxemburg predicted nearly a hundred years ago, the Labour leaders thus became not just milder and meeker fighters for the same aim, but ferocious opponents of all fighters.

Many Labour Party members who have followed the argument so far, and agreed with it, will now protest: 'We are not in the Labour Party to destroy campaigning. We are there to *change* the Labour Party and at the same time to support campaigners and strikers in their struggles.'

Such people are thin on the ground today, much thinner than they were ten years ago. In 1980, disgusted by the record of the 1974-9 Labour government, socialists in their thousands rallied to the banner of Tony Benn in his attempt to change the Labour Party. His 1981 campaign for the deputy leadership of the party attracted more socialists than any other campaign on the left of the party since the war. More flocked to his meetings than had gone to similar meetings addressed by Aneurin Bevan in the early 1950s, to the 'Victory for Socialism' campaign in the late 1950s or the 'Appeal for Unity' in the early 1960s. Probably 150,000 socialists actively supported Tony Benn in his campaign. Though Benn himself failed by the narrowest whisker to win the deputy leadership, huge strides were made to reform the Labour Party from within. The election of the leader was organised on much more democratic lines and Labour MPs were obliged to put themselves up for re-selection in each parliamentary term. The Young Socialists gained new strength and influence within the party.

Very quickly, this powerful movement evaporated. Some threw in their hand with the new Labour leader, Neil Kinnock. Others, far the majority, slunk off to nowhere. How could so many socialists disappear so fast? The answer is that for all their hostility to the right-wing Labour leadership, their central political strategy was the same: to change society from the top down, through a different and more socialist Labour Party—but nevertheless a party whose central strategy was to get elected to parliament and pass laws. For the supporters of Tony Benn in the early 1980s, therefore, the changing of the Labour Party was the first and last objective. They poured all their effort and enthusiasm into it.

While they did so, and almost without their noticing it, the working-class movement on the ground was beaten again and again in a series of terrible defeats. During the recession of the early 1980s two and a half million jobs were destroyed. Many of the sacked workers could have organised all kinds of protests, occupations or strikes. Some did so, though usually without success because the trade union leaders were unwilling to throw their weight behind the resistance. The huge rise of militancy in Labour conference halls took place against the background of a huge decline in militancy on the shop floor.

As a result, when defeat at the polls followed defeat for the unions, the Labour left was quite unprepared. Their changed Labour Party, with a comparatively left-wing programme, was trounced in the 1983 general election. A new Social Democratic Party, led by former right-wing Labour leaders and allied to the Liberal Party, got 26 per cent of the vote, compared to Labour's 28 per cent. The process was completed by the defeat of the miners' strike in 1985.

Since the chief field of operations for Benn's supporters was the Labour Party, and since the Labour Party plainly could not win an election without trimming its sails to fit the winds of defeat and stealing the right-wing clothes of the new SDP, there was suddenly nowhere for them to go. Many smartly changed their spots, and snuggled comfortably under the wing of the new leader, Neil Kinnock, who at once marched them off sharply to the right. Many others dropped out of politics altogether. Pretty well the only survivor was Tony Benn himself, who kept up his spirit and his socialism by abandoning any further ministerial ambition and, while still sticking to the Labour Party, turning his attentions more and more to stoking the fire down below.

The theme of this book is that fire down below. If society is to change in a socialist direction and if capitalism is to be replaced by socialism, the source of that change must be the fight against the exploitative society by the exploited people themselves. To knuckle down to the notion that changes can only come from the top is to accept the most debilitating and arrogant of all capitalist arguments: namely that there is at all times in human history a God-given élite, a few who are equipped to rule, while most people are not capable of government or politics and should count themselves lucky to have the occasional chance to choose which section of the élite should govern them.

This assumption of the rights of the few and the ignorance and inefficiency of the many is the hallmark of class rule through all our history. The reformer who believes that an educated elite in a parliament can change things for the masses, can—in the words of the Labour Party's famous Clause Four—'secure for the workers... the full fruits of their industry', is really playing the same game and making the same assumptions as the most bigoted class warrior. Both believe that whatever is right and wrong for most people can only be determined by the enlightened few.

That way there lies no prospect of any real change, and what changes are made that way will as likely as not be reversed by the same process. Real change, in people's attitudes as well as in reforms, comes only when people at the sharp end of exploitation organise and fight against it. To repeat yet again: the emancipation of labour, the one real hope for human civilisation, can only be achieved by the struggle for self-emancipation.

Socialists should align themselves with that struggle. They should organise themselves, their activity and their propaganda to sharpen the weapons against the old society and to build the confidence and strength of the minority who are prepared to fight.

Minority. There is the word which causes the most heated opposition. Surely, it is argued, socialism is about *majorities* being in charge of society. Surely the exploited billions are the majority in society—by far. How then can socialists argue that they should concern themselves with a minority rather than seek to get the support of majorities?

The answer is that the minority among whom socialists should organise is active, while the majority whose votes are canvassed at election times is passive. The passive majority is prey all the time to the machinations of class society, especially to its mass media. The active minority, because it is active, is capable of resisting those pressures, of responding to new ideas and creating their own.

The passive majority accept most of the time what they are told, what they read in the papers and see on television. There is a view, fashionable on the left for many years, that these media alone are responsible for people's reactionary ideas, that if only the media could be curbed, controlled or censored, people would think differently. In fact, people's reactionary ideas have their root in the way society is organised. Marx put it like this:

> The class which has the means of material production at its disposal has control at the same time over the means of mental production, so that, thereby, generally speaking, the ideas of those who lack the means of mental production are subject to it.

Thus, for instance, a favourite 'idea' among our ruling-class propagandists is 'freedom'. This freedom means the right to vote for a parliament, the right to say and even write what you like provided you can find a publisher or an audience. This freedom also means the right to make money from other people and the right to be enormously rich.

Great disparities of wealth in society, however, restrict freedoms every bit as much as restrictions on voting. Everyone is 'free' to send their children to private school, to have tea at the Ritz, to gamble on the stock exchange. These 'freedoms' are defended far more vigorously than the freedom to vote, yet they are in fact *restrictions* on freedom. For every one person who can have tea at the Ritz, there are a hundred who cannot do so because they have not got the money. If 10 per cent can send their children to private school and secure for them a straight route back into the privileged class from which they came, 90 per cent cannot do so—are banned from doing so—because they cannot afford it.

Thus the 'freedom' handed out by capitalist society is more often than not the opposite of freedom. Yet the *idea* of freedom still prevails, because the prevailing ideas of any society are the ideas of the class which runs it.

So the people who fight against these ideas—whether in strikes, demonstrations, popular protests or just in argument—are always, or almost always, swimming against the stream. They are the minority. But this minority, unlike the passive majority, can involve other people far outside their immediate orbit. And once involved in struggle against the old society, people's ideas can change decisively.

The Vietnam Solidarity Campaign in the 1960s, without any help from parliament or the passive majority, went a long way to changing people's attitudes to the Vietnam War. The Anti Nazi League in the 1970s, by organising among young people who were prepared to fight against fascism, rolled back a growing racist and fascist movement. The anti-poll tax movement today, boycotted by parliament, abused by Labour leaders and attacked by the police, brought hundreds of thousands of people into the battle against the tax by encouraging them not to pay it. In each of these cases and in countless others all over the world, active, fighting minorities have inspired real change in people's material conditions and in their ideas.

A fighting minority can do even more. As we saw in the section on the Russian revolution, it can become the majority. It was precisely because socialists were organised downwards, because a socialist party concentrated all its effort on the fighting spirit of the masses, that the Bolsheviks were able to win the *soviets* from the Mensheviks and in doing so to win the hearts and minds of the majority of the Russian working class. In such circumstances, and only in such circumstances, can capitalist society ever be ended and replaced by a socialist society. The fighting minorities become ruling majorities only in a revolution.

Revolution? Is that not a distant and even a ridiculous idea in the last decade of the 20th century? Is it not something which happened 200 years ago in France and 70 years ago in Russia, but is hardly even thinkable today?

The answer is that there have been as many revolutionary situations in the past twenty-five years as in any other quarter century in history. In France in 1968, for instance, there was a students' revolt and a general strike which for an instant threatened one of the most powerful and complacent ruling classes in the world. In 1974 there was a revolution in Portugal. In 1979 there was a revolution in Iran. In 1981, as we have seen, the workers of Poland came within a whisker of bringing down the regime. In all these four cases, the whole structure of class power was in jeopardy. In each case, a new system of society, a socialist system, was made possible by the revolutionary actions of the masses.

In each case the masses were defeated. The revolutionary wave subsided, and society slid back into reaction. There was nothing inevitable about this. What was missing in all four upheavals was a strong organisation of socialists linked to the fighting spirit of the working class.

The vast majority of socialists in all four countries had organised as they had done elsewhere, basing themselves either on a parliamentary strategy or on the local Communist party and state-capitalist Russia. In a revolutionary situation both forms of organisation proved weak, almost helpless. Unable, unwilling and unused to moving forward with the masses, they sought allies and strategies which handed the initiative back to reaction. Leaderless, and without a strategy to take them forward to a new society, the masses slowed down the pace of the struggle. In France and Portugal the beneficiaries were the old social-democratic parties and the Communist parties, in Iran the fanatical and superstitious *mullahs*, in Poland the armed forces of the state-capitalist war machine.

In revolutionary circumstances, a relatively small group of organised revolutionary socialists who have linked themselves, in good times and in bad, with the struggle at the bottom of society can make the difference as to whether the revolution goes on to change the old society or retreats to shore it up again.

Socialism is, and must always be, a revolutionary idea. Unless it means the transfer of economic power from a small, greedy and irresponsible élite to the democratic control of the majority it means nothing. Since this transfer will not willingly be conceded, it can take place only in a revolution. So socialists must be revolutionaries. They have to organise themselves and direct their propaganda in the only area where there is any real prospect of change: among the minority who are prepared to fight. Their success is measured not by their ideological purity, still less by their propensity to rant and hector, but by their ability to organise and encourage people who do not share all their ideas but who are ready to fight.

This minority may change from year to year, week to week. The dynamics of class society are always throwing up new struggles, usually in unexpected areas, where people who imagined themselves law-abiding and decent citizens suddenly find themselves indignantly fighting against the rulers they previously respected. The presence and organisation of socialists in such circumstances can be crucial to victory or defeat. The chief job of socialists is to spread and link the struggles across the boundaries of race, sex, religion and nation.

The militant coal miner, for instance, sees the import of coal from abroad as a threat and is inclined to call for import controls. The socialist coal miner, however, can point to other socialist coal miners in South Africa, Poland, the United States, Russia—and make common cause with them. Similarly, militant workers are often distracted by racist arguments. They accept at once that there are too many people in this country and that black people should be kept out. Socialist workers can establish the links between white and black workers; can point out that the immigrant is just another worker shoved about as a pawn on the capitalist board in just the same way as British workers are.

Unafraid of losing votes and determined only to pursue socialist ideas, socialists who organise among the fighting minority can say what they think, and act accordingly. Their politics are different in style and content from the necessarily opportunistic and usually racist and nationalist claptrap of those who hunt for votes from the passive majority. They can speak out against the sexism which pollutes so much of working-class life, stand up for gay people, seek a solution to the 'Irish question' by demanding that Britain clear out of Ireland where it has caused nothing but dissension and pain for 400 years.

In all these matters and countless others which arise in conversation and in experience every day of the week, cautious and careerist politicians prefer to stand aside with a shy smile or a shrug—in the fear that any intervention on any 'unpopular' issue might lose them votes. The result of course is that racism, sexism, nationalism—and all the other 'isms' fed by the Tory press to divide and humiliate us—fester and grow.

Here is the main point one last time.

Socialism means nothing unless it means control of society from below. There is no hope of achieving that socialism except by action from below. For most of the twentieth century the idea of socialism has been poisoned by people who pretend that it can be instituted from on high: by well-meaning parliamentarians or by blind or brutal Stalinists. Now the Labour parliamentarians, in their rush for votes, are rapidly abandoning the word 'socialism' —the idea itself they abandoned long ago. Stalinism is dead. The 'growing wrath' against a system which has brought the world to the rim of hell is everywhere: in furious strikes in South Korea, in courageous uprisings of the oppressed Palestinians in the Middle East, in a new impatient fury at the wrecking of the world's environment, in anti-poll tax demonstrations all over Britain.

There has never been a time when socialism—real socialism, socialism from below, socialism whose main ingredient is democracy, socialism won by fighting against capitalism—is more relevant. There is a world to win, and it is time for socialists to shake off their inhibitions, and go out to organise where it can be won.

SWP

Join the Socialist Workers Party

Socialism, the emancipation of the working class, is the act of the working class. That is why the Socialist Workers Party is a party of activists, seeking always for the point at which our effort will carry us one step further on the road to socialism.

We appeal to all who agree with us to join us.

If you can only go with us part of the way, then work with us for our common goal.

Write to the National Office, Socialist Workers Party, PO Box 82, London E3 3LH. (For a list of revolutionary socialist organisations in other countries, see the early pages of this book).

Read Socialist Worker...

...the weekly newspaper of the SWP, with up-to-date news and analysis from the workers' movement throughout the world.

Available every week through your local SWP branch —or for a special introductory subscription of the next ten issues, sent to you post free, send £3.00 to Socialist Worker Circulation Department, PO Box 82, London E3 3LH.

Books and pamphlets on socialism

Arguments for revolutionary socialism / *John Molyneux*
What about human nature? Isn't the real problem overpopulation? Surely we have to defend the national interest? This book sets out the socialist answers to everyday questions. 128 pages. £2.50 / $4.75

How Marxism works / *Chris Harman*
The basic ideas of Marxism explain, as no other set of ideas can, the contradiction-wracked society in which we live. This is a beginner's guide—clear and readable. 96 pages. £1.95 / $3.50

The future socialist society / *John Molyneux*
We offer no 'blueprint' for a socialist society—socialist democracy means the mass of workers will themselves decide its shape. But we can set out the socialist vision, as this pamphlet does. 32 pages. £0.95 / $1.75

The revolutionary ideas of Karl Marx / *Alex Callinicos*
'The philosophers have merely interpreted the world; the point, however, is to change it,' said Marx. His explanations of the world we live in give us a firm footing when we start to push. 208 pages. £3.95 / $7.95

Russia: How the revolution was lost / *Chris Harman*
Why was the great potential of the Russian revolution strangled by a new bureaucratic ruling class and a new dictator, Stalin? This pamphlet gives a short account of these crucial events. 32 pages. £1.00 / $1.75

State capitalism in Russia / *Tony Cliff*
The original exposition of the theory of state capitalism, which for the first time explained the nature of Russia under Stalin. Not an easy read, but worth the effort. 377 pages. £5.95 / $12.00

Russia: From workers' state to state capitalism
/ Peter Binns, Tony Cliff and Chris Harman
What road led from a workers' revolution to a bureaucratic state? This book offers hard answers to tough questions. 112 pages. £2.50 / $4.75

Class struggles in Eastern Europe 1945-83 / *Chris Harman*
A vivid account of the upheavals that have shaken the Eastern bloc in the past 40 years—struggles which show the potential of the workers' movement in the clashes yet to come. 382 pages. £7.95 / $13.50

The Labour Party: A Marxist history
/ Tony Cliff and Donny Gluckstein
Labour has the passive support of millions of workers. This book judges the party according to its own pretensions to be their standard-bearer, from Keir Hardie to Neil Kinnock. 430 pages. £7.95 / $13.50

Women and perestroika / *Chanie Rosenberg*
The changing conditions for women in Russia—under the Tsar, the 1917 revolution, Stalin and Gorbachev—are a touchstone by which to judge the effects of *perestroika* for all workers. 128 pages. £3.95 / $7.50

The Fire last time: 1968 and after / *Chris Harman*
1968: battles with the police on the streets of Paris, Russian tanks in Prague, ghetto risings in the USA. This book looks at the contradictions of the system that led to these upheavals. 416 pages. £6.95 / $13.50

All these books and pamphlets are available from branch bookstalls of the Socialist Workers Party, from bookshops, or by post from Bookmarks (add 10 per cent to cover postage—minimum 35p or $1).

BOOKMARKS
265 Seven Sisters Road, London N4 2DE, England.
PO Box 16085, Chicago, IL 60616, USA.
GPO Box 1473N, Melbourne 3001, Australia.

Bookmarks bookshop in London runs a large socialist mail order service. We have stocks of books and pamphlets on socialism, internationalism, trade union struggle, women's issues, economics, working-class history, the Marxist classics and much, much more. We will send books anywhere in the world. Write for our latest booklists to:
BOOKMARKS
265 Seven Sisters Road, London N4 2DE, England.